# COMEDY TONIGHT

**Selective Film Guide**

William Russo

# LONG TIME AGO BOOKS

Imprint: Independently published
ISBN: 9798699136681

On cover: top row: Walter Matthau, Elaine May, Lou Costello, Charles Laughton, Marilyn Monroe, Jack Benny, Rod Steiger.
Bottom row:  Charlie Chaplin, Spider Man, Brent Spinner, Patrick Stewart, Sean Connery, Tarantula.

# Comedy Reviews

Over the past  ten years, if you had asked me, I would say there were few comedies I reviewed.  Reasons?  Mostly because I was often critical of humor more than other movie styles, yet I often wrote humorous pieces and satiric barbs. I never like finding a movie is terrible and unfunny. It is such a waste of previous time with so many thousands of movies to see. Perhaps that caused me to be hypercritical. In fact, some of my nastiest reviews are reserved for the comedy field.

Yet, when I went through the collection, I was surprised at how many I did watch and how many I did like. There are some gems in here for sure. And, there are more than I would have guessed.

Though my humor runs toward Noel Coward and mannered satire, there are a few outlandish screwball films here. There are also some that were never intended to be funny, but seemed to have a funny bone in the head.

We hope you find this mishmash entertaining. We decided not to categorize or put in any particular order. Chaos is often the hallmark of humor. We also decided against an index. You should be surprised and miffed, unsure of what's next. That is the hallmark of life in an age of pandemics, regenerated racial supremacists, and political upheaval.

This book answers the question on whether the critic can be funnier than the movie.

# Dr. William Russo

## First Bond

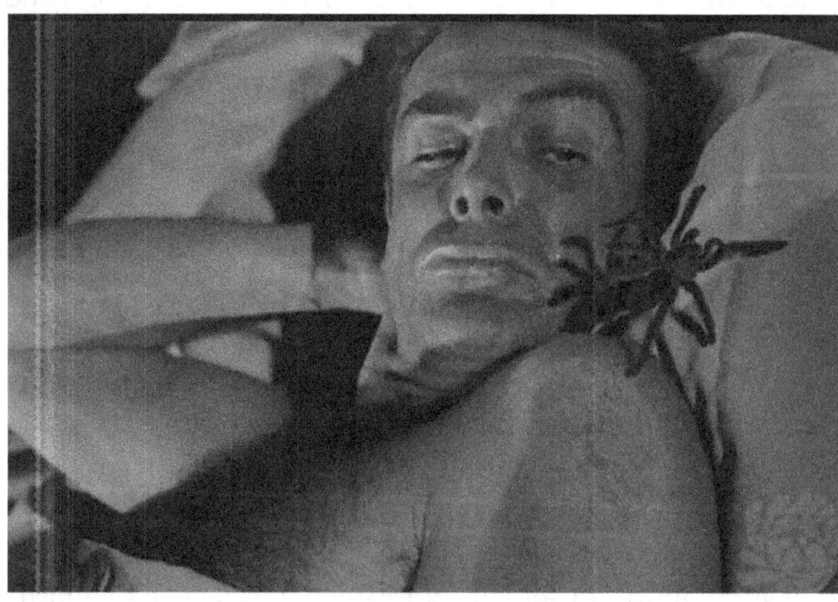

Back in 1963, audiences were treated to a new kind of superhero in the person of Sean Connery:  Bond, James Bond.

The film called *Dr. No* was a departure on many levels from your usual spy/adventure stories. First, this was tongue-in-cheek (sort of) and came out of a series of Cold War novels by Ian Fleming. It is hilarious in many respects.

As you might expect in this movie, the spies are decidedly low tech: old fashioned telephone banks are everywhere. There are no computers, and MI-5 or 6 communicates by short-wave radio with its agents.

The shocker: Bond has a license to kill and does so with the aplomb of your everyday cold-blooded sociopath. Of course, it's all done in the name of the Queen and Country.

This movie deals with an independent terrorist organization that calls itself SPECTRE and is motivated mostly by evil and money, whichever is most handy.

The movie is lusciously filmed in Technicolor in Jamaica where Dr. No (Joseph Wiseman), a half-Chinese mad genius, has a nuclear power plant where his workers wear what we'd call Hazmat suits today. Yet, the whole bunch of bananas seems like parody, not far from *Get Smart.* The role was offered to Noel Coward, but he shockingly turned it down.

Along for the Bond ride in this first Fleming novel on the big screen is Ursula Andress in various stages of undress and Jack Lord as the CIA agent (before he went *Hawaii 5-O* on us). Wiseman's half-Chinese villain has no hands (black prosthetics) and cream-color suits that would make Sydney Greenstreet envious.

Bond is nothing less than promiscuous and rather dangerous, and Connery is perfect as the pre-politically-correct man's man. Don't shake that martini. Audiences must have hooted every time that Bond music motif hit the screen. It still tingles.

We particularly like the tarantula put into Bond's bed and crawling up Connery's arm and back. Ah, those were the days!

## Android Data Plays Sherlock in Satire!

In the second season of *Star Trek the Next Generation,* two of the costar characters (Data, the Android and Geordi, the blind officer) go to the Hologram room in the starship to take on roles as Sherlock and Watson, as a lark.

Their knowledge of the Conan Doyle canon is impressive, but the computer Hologram throws them a few curve balls.

It would seem to be an easy question as to who would play whom. As a team, the two characters seemed to be based on a minor-league parody of Holmes and Watson. It was, we think, intended to be light and facetious or a change of pace.

One of the ship's doctors (Diana Muldaur) speaks out that she believes Data (Brent Spinner) cannot solve a case as he is android and incapable of human deductions. His friend Geordi (Levar Burton) is intrigued, and the three re-enter the Hologram that is hijacked (unknown to them) by Prof. Moriarty. This action means a fictional character may do damage to the Star Trek Enterprise computer system.

Moriarty becomes aware that he is an energy form, but not a life form, merely fictional. The debate between Captain Picard ((Patrick Stewart) may be fascinating, well beyond elementary. Daniel Davis is the American actor who plays off Data and learns in his 19th century personage how to run a 24th century computer system.

This was a worthy testament to the Sherlock *oeuvre.* The episode gave enough philosophical fireworks to fill a short TV show, having an abrupt conclusion to what appeared to be a major conundrum.

Add block

## Bruce Weber's Boys

Bruce Weber, as a film-maker and fashionista, made a career of studying masculinity in all its forms. He started with a young boxing coach named Andy Minsker and his latest is a bio-doc about Robert Mitchum.

This documentary is odd in a funny way.

In between during his long career, Weber has run into the wall of many from his generation: the values and relationships with male models he created in the beginning have not held up to today's more overly sensitive accusers.

Yes, Bruce Weber has suffered charges of sexual harassment from a dozen or more men who might have let it slide years ago. Today, money-struck and fame-driven revenge pulls these guys into a world of accusations, both dubious and false.

In Weber's first movie, *Broken Noses,* he took on a lookalike to jazz beauty Chet Baker. This young man, born in 1982, had been a teenage boxing champ—and coached other adolescents in how to box.
Today with horrors over concussions and other masculine pursuits deemed too violent, that world of homoerotic attraction is far more dangerous for other reasons, like being a Boy Scout leader.

Minsker was adorable, charming, and could likely win followers with his easy-going personality. His image on T-shirts from youth still may bring him fame. Weber made him into a book of photos—and relentless celebrity.

The film in black and white from 1987 is hypnotic and staggering to think it could never be made today. Even back then, the Olympic people warned boys to avoid Weber. Andy Minsker was utterly intrigued by the alarms and pursued Weber.

Interestingly, Weber next went on to do a film *Let's Get Lost* on Chet Baker right before the jazz great met a hideous end.

As for *Broken Noses,* you might see more than the surface and inclinations in that regard are like reading Tarot cards. You may see something insightful, or you may just go off the deep end. These young adolescents were part of a norm for the 1980s, and they were the last of a breed. Soon political correctness and re-defined masculine codes would end this world of seductive youth.

Weber's career has its notoriety and its sublime beauty, and to see *Broken Noses* thirty years later is like looking at an extinct animal in the wild.

You may fall out of the orbit of Weber's men and boys, but you cannot deny his sociological and psychological truisms.

## Cabot & Price Stifle Their Laughs!

Nathaniel Hawthorne's mid-nineteenth century short stories were collected by him into a book, with more than a dozen philosophical mysteries. It was titled *Twice Told Tales*. He was not into the psychological terror as his fellow writer, Edgar Allen Poe.

There is an almost pre-science fiction quality to his literary themes, and yet when they were adapted for the big screen in 1963, the star and narrator of the film would be Vincent Price, already a big name in bad literary adaptations.

Price found steady work doing high-end schlock for more than a few decades. He brought dignity and style to what might normally pass for low-budget pot-boilers. Twice Told Tales

zeroes in on three stories (two are famous in their own rights:  "Dr. Heidegger's Experiment" and "Rappuccini's Daughter"). The third story in the trilogy-anthology is *House of Seven* Gables, which was a novel, his usual *métier.*
Two center on scientists who play God, trying to control human nature and life over death. In the first, Dr. Heidegger's tale is altered seriously. It becomes a small cast melodrama, now set in a dark and stormy night. Sebastian Cabot and Price are aging in pursuit of the Fountain of Youth.

 In "Rappaccini's Daughter," he is a reclusive scientist who has filled his daughter with poison from a plant to make her separate from the normal business of social life. These are changed enough to be slick color TV specials of the era: about forty minutes each.

*House of Seven Gables* is another known title, but hardly within the themes of the first two. Here, a house holds a mysterious presence of evil, rather than the people which include an heir played by Price again.  Richard Denning and Beverly Garland join him in this ghostly tale of hidden treasure.
They are not horrific much, slow-moving, and quite literary, hardly up to contemporary standards of horror and special effects. That may be their charm. If you want something that is neither the original Hawthorne story, nor a modern flashy horror, this is your movie.

## HITCHCOCK'S LAMB

Reportedly one of Hitchcock's favorite episodes of his show *Hitchcock Presents*,  he directed his old friend Barbara Bel Geddes again. She had the thankless role of the loyal and unrequited love of Scottie in *Vertigo.* For all her dedication to taking care of him, she picks up the dregs at the end (we presume she has little enough self-respect).

It is wickedly funny.

In the "Lamb to the Slaughter," she plays a pregnant woman whose callous policeman husband drops by their quaint little bungalow home to give her his notice that he has found another woman.

This biting irony was written by Raold Dahl who also gave us Willie Wonka. Not quite the factory of Fun time here.

The presumable victim entitled to be more than mousy over this last straw, we have not seen enough to draw conclusions. But, the victim is Barbara Bel Geddes, and she is nice.

However, for those looking for clues, the first few seconds of the show are telling. The pregnant woman tosses a wrapper carelessly over her shoulder, as if she were a slob at heart in her spotless little home.

We know better. She realizes in a few minutes one more piece of trash on the floor will not be noticed by the visitors she expects after she dispatches her husband with a frozen leg of lamb on the noggin.

After messing up the house like a struggle has occurred, she goes out to the local supermarket to pick up a few healthy vegetables. She puts the leg of lamb in the oven and starts cooking it.

Her sly passive-aggressive plan has colleagues of her husband investigate his odd death, though they know he plays around on a pregnant woman. They are in sympathy—and so the audience even when they see a premeditated murder.

Hitchcock has made the fetus an accomplice in the murder. It is Hitchcock's nasty business at his most humorous.

## JACK THE TAILOR OF BEVERLY HILLS

**Clothes Make the Man!**

Upon first coming across a one-hour documentary on a fashion store in Beverly Hills, we thought it was one of those vanity documentaries, produced by its subject. Jack Taylor was a 90-year old high fashion artist from old Hollywood days.

The film is a tad old, with Taylor gone in 2016 and his main supporter, Mike Douglas, a decade before that. Yet, we are always eager to catch up on our past misgivings.

Jack Taylor hardly needs publicity, and business is dying out as his A-list celebrity patrons pass away. He would soon follow and take an era with him. He was the man who tailored all those magnificent suits worn by Cary Grant from the 1930s till his death. Grant would order a dozen suits at time.

We wondered if there were any celebs who'd go on camera for a commercial appearance—and there were plenty of men: Mike Douglas, Hal Linden, swore by Jack Taylor. Monty Hall wore a different outfit every show on Let's Make a Deal, all created by Taylor.

He made clothes for Elvis, Sinatra, Charles Bronson, and so many men. He was not easy either. He would tell them not to eat or put on weight. His suits were meant to show them off at their best shape. His most obstreperous client was Jackie Gleason who needed 3 sizes, because of his weight changes over weeks and months.

Taylor would tell them to eat only half the plate at the restaurant. He did not do alterations, or sew the suits. He has a 60-year tailor for that: he has worked for Taylor for sixty years. He's in his 80s. But both lament there are no tailors any longer.

We are looking at the extinction of men's fashion. There was no endangered species list: men's suits and ties were dinosaurs when the political landscape changed its pants.

Clothes for men nowadays are off the rack at best, and China imports at worst. Jack Taylor knows his world of well-dressed men is fading away. He thinks the 1940s were the last gasp, but the war killed it at that point. And, the 1970s turned into a fashion death knell for men's clothing with jeans and t-shirts as the extent of wardrobe.

We never expected to be fascinated at expensive clothes, being a recluse who never makes public appearances. However, celebrities still know a good suit is essential, but they are going to have a hard time finding anyone to replace jack Taylor.

## An Innocent Age

Back in 1953 for the first show of his second season, Jack Benny garnered the biggest name and biggest star of the year: Marilyn Monroe. It was called the *Jack Benny Program*.

As all the set-ups in the Benny program were at the expense of Jack's delicate ego, he took the barrage of raps and insults with his usual aplomb.

You might be ready for some outdated racial profiling when Rochester showed up: Eddie Anderson always played Jack's valet who goes with him everywhere and calls him "Boss." Here they go to Hawaii, and we find Jack lugging all the luggage with no Rochester.

Jack sits on the dock, ready to leave, while flower leis are given to all the departing guests for their generosity, kindness, and friendship. Alas, even a dog gets a lei, but not Jack. Finally a delicatessen owner shows up and gives him a lei of chicken livers. He is warned to be careful of the seagulls.

We learn too that Jack is carrying Rochester's luggage because he was late for the ship.

When Benny falls asleep on deck, he dreams about the star he saw that night in a ship's nightly movie: *Gentlemen Prefer Blondes* megastar, Marilyn Monroe.   And, in one of her designer gowns, she drops into the Barcalounger recliner next to Jack in his dreams.

She professes her love for him despite their age difference. She points out she is 25 and he is 39, but in 25 years she will be 50, and he will still be 39. She is enchanted by his big blue eyes.

It was Monroe's first TV appearance as a guest star (we don't count her TV commercials, satirized in *All About Eve*).  She is lovely and charming, and so is Jack.

You simply don't have that kind of weekly series surprise, even with cable nowadays. It was a gentle treat of a bygone era, and a lovely little escape from today.

## Vampire Classic from 1980s

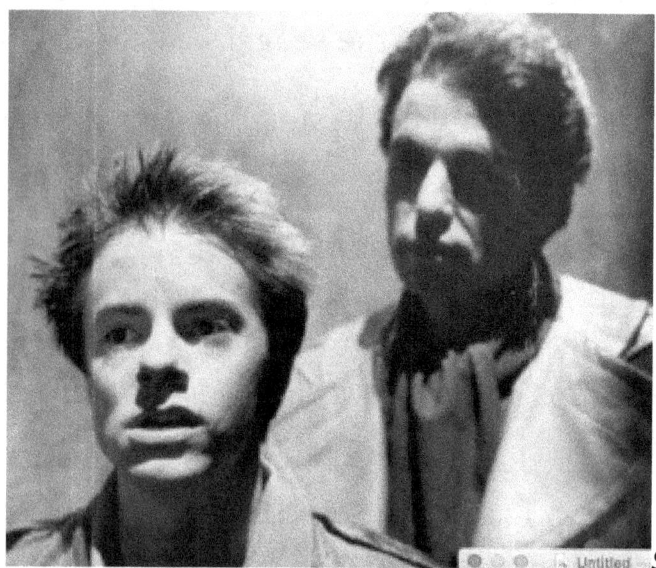


*Sarandon & Jeffreys*

Has it really been 35 years since *Fright Night* rejuvenated modern vampires?

It was Tom Holland who wrote and directed it, looking like a B-movie for TV show of the week, apart from the nudity now and then. By today's cable movie standards, this is rough, however still holds up as entertainment with a modern twist.

Two points of amusement remain unflappable: Roddy MacDowell and Stephen Jeffreys. They survive in name for sheer wacky performances. MacDowell plays an aging movie star who used to play vampire hunters in his heyday, and Jeffreys plays a teenage Jack Nicholson on uppers. He later reneged Hollywood to do gay adult films for a while, though that is now denied with a half-baked story that it was his evil twin brother.

The vampire is demure and stately Chris Sarandon, looking like he wandered into the wrong California suburb. Yes, the vampire has taken a house in a *Leave It to Beaver* part of town where you can peer into the next-door windows. It seems like he's asking for teenage trouble.

Stephen Jeffreys steals the big scenes: he becomes clearly the gay victim of Sarandon's vampire. His two delicious scenes are with Roddy as they battle.

For MacDowell with his hair fake-frosted, this was a last grand role, and he makes the most of it. Director Holland was lucky to have the veteran star in his movie.

There is no scrimping on special effects at the finish, and you have a sunny California vampire tale.

The film was originally set to star Vincent Price, not McDowall, and Anthony Michael Hall, not Jeffreys. And, we still haven't figured out what Sarandon's boyfriend is supposed to be.

In the whatever happened mode, William Ragsdale is the star juvenile lead. He's cookie-cutter good enough. Yet, he is thrown up against two scene-stealing actors who rob him of the movie. The film is considered a classic nowadays.

## Wild West Satire with John Wayne

*Not Laurel & Hardy!*

Back in the 1950s when John Wayne was the number one box office attraction, it was a treat if he made a guest appearance on TV. The series is called *Forsaken Westerns* and features a plethora of deplorable episodes with Michael Landon, Leonard Nimoy, and many others before they made it big.

One of those syndicated series that collects odd-ball appearances of noted TV stars when they were unknown in lost pilot episodes, has also brought us a true peculiar and weird little dollop:  John Wayne in a satiric, overextended TV skit called *The Northwest Killer,* in which Duke Wayne is falsely accused of murder and hunted down by a relentless RCMP Mountie.

Now this is supposed to be comedy, a throwaway extended bit for a variety show in 1959. The host of the show is none other than the irrepressible Jimmy Durante.

Yes, Durante, the Schnoze, plays a variation of Sgt. Preston of the Yukon, in his Mountie outifit, red jacket lost in black and white. Durante marches around and pivots to Wayne's amusement as he plays unlucky Pierre, trapped in bad TV comedy

This is probably 15 minutes of most excruciating and unfunny bits, done like a multi-scene Western ever put on TV. There are several fistfights between Durante and Duke—and hilariously (we supposed) Durante bests the box-office champ. Wayne turns to the camera and promises the kids, "I win the next fight."

Of course, being funny was secondary here: the treat was to see Jimmy Durante and John Wayne in a western satire. It has all the promise and none of the quality you'd hope. Pratfalls are outrageous, and Wayne likely enjoyed doing some comedy as a change of pace. Also on the bill is a guest appearance of Gary Cooper with Jack Benny, equally unfunny, in which Benny in high-heeled boots is the same height at Coop. He nearly falls over several times and is rescued, unscripted, by the laconic Gary Cooper.

It was a surprise to find such stuff after 50 years, and the ghosts of Wayne and Cooper likely wish they had lost these horrors permanently.

## Mae West, Way Ahead of the Curve!

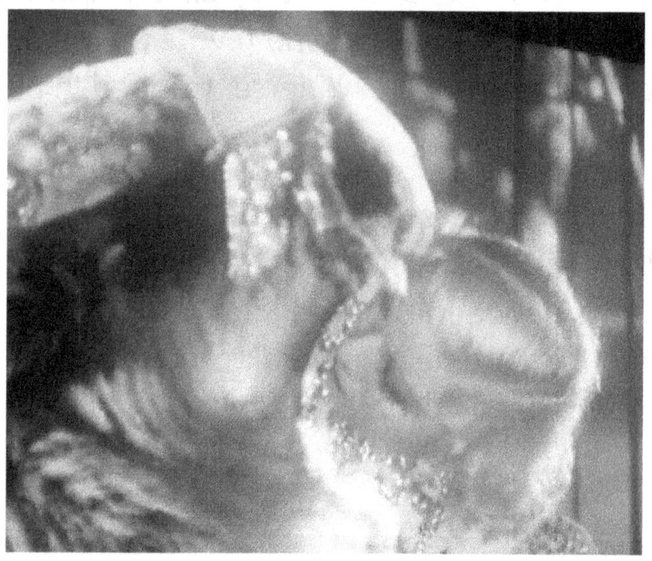

*Mae in Lion's Mouth!*

When PBS Masters finally recognizes Mae 100 years after her astounding Broadway run, you know she is still years ahead of the rest of society. How did this woman whose first plays were called "garbage," or "lewd" or worse, manage to transcend *Sex* and *The Drag* to become a *sotto voce* comic?

She was hardly a dirty blonde, but she was stunning to behold.

Her first play about a sex worker resulted in a week-long jail sentence that became the best publicity stunt New Yorkers ever saw. Her second play, she scoured the drag queen bars of the 1920s to find 60 gay men and women to do her ground-breaking shocker about homosexuality!

It took her thinking about why few women attended her plays (she wrote, directed, and starred). So, she came up with Diamond Lil, in hour-glass dresses, fancy lingerie, and big hats: add a few off-hand jokes, and she was Mae West forever.

You could say she saved Paramount Studios with her astute performances: she was in charge of everything and made $1 more than the highest paid executive. She insisted on black performers with billing in her movies, and she gave Duke Ellington his first Hollywood exposure!

Mae hated negativity—and she liked to be in control. Slowly she evolved into a real version of her creative version. She was forty and overweight when she made her first movie, and she was run out of Hollywood by censors. By the 1950s, she was considered a man in drag herself--and she was ripe for parody everywhere.

In the 1970s in her 80s, she made a comeback as a sex symbol, a shocking parody that was hilarious in *Sextette* and *Myra Breckinridge*. With her half-baked singing, shimmy, and snide overcurrent delivery, she was a striking original.

## Literary Road Trips

*Steve Coogan with Rob Brydon.*

With great sadness we are saying goodbye to the highly intelligent, witty, charming series of movies with Steve Coogan and Rob Brydon. Their last is *The Trip to Greece,* all four civilized comedies were directed by Michael Winterbottom.

These have been four rarities of the modern age: witty as Noel Coward, beautifully locations, with amusing company. And they aren't even gay. Two performers whose competition extends to out-imitating the other are sent on a fictional outing. Their job as journalists is to visit fine restaurants and write reviews.

The actors sort of play themselves in Brydon and Coogan (notable Oscar nominee for Stan and Ollie, as he was Stan). You often cannot tell where the fiction starts, as they play versions of themselves blending over into plot contrivance. Their litany of impersonations (Brando, Hoffman, Olivier, Caine, Pacino, Jagger) makes for a variety of dinner companions.

Four films feature hilarious riffs and impersonations over dinner and while driving around luscious countryside in Greece. Brydon sings the tune from *Grease*, and he crunches it to fit the country. Coogan is dutifully appalled.

They transform imitations of Laurel and Hardy over lunch into breath-taking jokes: Oliver Hardy morphs into Tom Hardy.

These little forays to gourmet restaurants have a price in this film (350 Euros).

The bittersweet last entry in the series showcases the performers to their greatest wish: Brydon becomes the epitome of the light comedian—and Coogan, as he likes, becomes the tragic actor of Shakespearean levels.

Their frictions and battles are nothing short of delightful wordplay. You don't see that much anywhere in movies nowadays.

After visits to England, Italy, and Spain, this lap around the Aegean ends with a whimper. Brilliantly done, and hopefully there will be one more trip.

## Another Sequel, not *Deja Vu*

No, you didn't read this movie review last week here.

What more can you ask?  Beautiful scenery, lovely music, and witty conversation. Yes, those two British actors (one with 2 Oscar nominations) are back to delight us.

We have skipped the second trip to Italy for now and cut to the chase with *Trip to Spain.* These two marvelous performers can hit the road and still hit their marks. This is another follow up to their British series, *The Trip*, condensed and made into a feature film. No, it's not a mid-life crisis movie, despite what the *New York Times* claims.

They seem to make the films every three or four years, which is just about right. They are reality-based, as the stars play themselves, notable thespians and comedians on a journalistic journey for the New York Times as food critics, or culture commentators.

With each stop at a breathtaking locale, Steve Coogan foams at the mouth with his erudite knowledge. Heaven help you if you know more or have enough. Rob Brydon can match him every mile, and that makes them chemically compatible.

Each morsel is back-lit with some of the funniest conversations this side of reality. Coogan notes how sorry he feels for anyone who thinks this stuff is not scripted and fully ad-libbed. It's likely a circle within a square is outlined and the two drop in their witticisms.

However, the impressions make all the difference over the meals. When they argue over who does the best Mick Jagger impression as he plays Hamlet, you have moments that will knock fans of Noel Coward into the aisle.

Coogan remains prickly, but Brydon manages to break him up several times this trip, which may not have been planned.

If Coogan reminds us of ourselves, then we have had a bittersweet lesson. Sheer delight awaits the viewer.

## Coogan & Brydon in Italy

*The Trip to Italy* is the middle piece of the trilogy of mockumentaries by Steve Coogan and Rob Brydon. *The Trip to Italy* is directed by Michael Winterbottom again, and he condenses the film to the best *bon mot st*uttered during the two-week business holiday.

These minor British TV stars are on the verge of making it big in American movies, and they are thrown together for another series of adventures by the media. They are temperamental actors who seem not to enjoy each other's company.

However, they are amusing together. It's said that Abbot and Costello were not friends but were a business association. So, it is here. This is the business of growing older with wit and aplomb.

The conceit of the journey is to visit great Italian restaurants and trace the expatriates Byron and Shelley along the way.

Coogan and Brydon compete over everything, especially to show which one has more talent and is more successful. They do imitations of Hugh Grant, Roger Moore, Michael Caine, and Sean Connery, over dinners to die for in exotic coastal Italian tourist spots.

Not much is sacred here in their barbs, not even the dead at Pompeii.

You may not be used to intelligent conversation like this. You certainly wonder how they could not enjoy their mid-life crises while living *La Dolce Vita*.

Not everything is fun, as there is a downbeat inner core to the cavorting. They might die happy in one of these spots, but we doubt it. They sabotage their own trip, their friendship, and seem to have a grand time of indifference, their personal existential crises.

We are happy to have a chance to be a fly on the walls of their discontent.

## Boon Companions

*Gourmet Wit & Impersonations on the menu!*

We don't know how we missed this film or its sequels. We are delighted to say we have found them now: epicurean wit and breathtaking scenery.

Two minor actors for reasons unclear are assigned to sample fancy restaurants in northern England. You may well ask if there any fancy restaurants in far-off south of Scotland. You may well ask yourself why two actors would be hired as journalists, not even TV journalists.

Yet, this light fare is sweet enough and fluffy around the edges. Steve Coogan is often insufferable and hardly worthy of spending five days in a long car ride. Rob Brydon is more pleasant and funnier. We do vote that Steve's Michael Caine impersonation is better.

They have an edgy friendship, Platonic as Steve claims, but Coogan is known for his gay-themed movies like *Philomena* and *Ideal Home.* Here, he plays himself: as a womanizing aging actor.

There are some hilarious moments in a largely improvised script. One wonders why Brydon would be willing to go along after being told that just about everyone else said, no, thanks.

After an hour with Coogan, we understand why everyone from ex-wives to children and girlfriends are loathed to go anywhere with him. Alexander Pope's wit likely rendered him unpleasant too. Groucho's did.

They eat delectable meals and seem to have no appreciation for the hard work that goes into their menu trivia.

They sing-along during boring rides in the countryside, and they stop off in famous literary haunts. Their witty impersonations of notable and not-so-notable British stars (Michael Caine, Sean Connery, yes; Michael Sheen, no) are lively and funny.

Ultimately, Brydon admits that Coogan was exactly what he expected during their trip, and Coogan turns down a chance to star in an American TV series about a British pathologist.

How much is reality? How much is fake? Well, they made a few sequels—and we will sign up to go along with them.

Coogan insists it is not reality at all. It is the epitome of entertainment.

## Androgynous Villains

Keanu Reeves is hilarious as the hitman in *John Wick 2*. If you don't believe this movie is a comedy, you have no sense of the ridiculous.

We lost track of how many people Wick kills at the Caracalla Baths, among other notable settings. It becomes utterly preposterous amid the stunning scenery. We also enjoyed a shootout in the subway with silencers so that the bustling crowds have no idea the hitmen are trying to do each other in.

Of course, one of the great set pieces is the *homage*, or parody, of Orson Welles's mirror shootout in *Lady from Shanghai,* done here in super-exaggeration.

We are also bemused by the various androgynous killers after Keanu, especially the so-called woman (Ruby Rose) posing as a boyish killer. We laughed at Reeves buying guns at a secret shoppe like he was ordering bottles of wine for a big party.

The film is a flamboyant hoot, populated by a bunch of cameo star roles, from John Leguizamo to Laurence Fishburne and Ian McShane.

When Keanu walks down those streets of New York City, he discovers nearly every other person on the street is a professional hitman. It defies anything but laughter.

Wick is a sentimental guy who goes bananas when his dog is killed, or his car is stolen with a birthday card in the glovebox from his deceased girlfriend.

This is a big, glossy picture, filled with set pieces set around the globe with Keanu as some kind of mobster version of Jason Bourne.

We generally don't like killings, car chases, and explosions. Yes, the film does seem to go too far with a nightclub massacre, reminiscent of the Pulse club down in Florida last year.

Other than that, the violence becomes so mindless that you figure it is like watching the latest news reports about mass shootings in *(you name the location)*. No one blames these kind of movies nowadays for glorifying violence, or inspiring a view that life is cheap and easy to throw away.

*John Wick Chapter 2* is merely a symptom of the world we live in today. Laugh it off.

## Lost Satire

In the 1940s movies drew its fledgling stars from the ranks of radio comedians—like Bob Hope, Jack Benny, and in 1944, they called upon sharp satirist Fred Allen. Barely recalled nowadays, he came upon the movie world as an unlikely iconoclast, especially during the patriotic days of World War II.

Yes, in the world of major studios, to have someone biting the hand that feeds him was a rare event. *It's in the Bag* was middle-aged, baggy-eyed Allen's debut on the big screen.

Allen rakes American foibles over the coals with the best of them—and it was a strange treat to see small-time American business, intellectuals, politics, lawyers, police, hotels, and middle-class morality under siege.

Allen takes on greed in America as his main target. He plays a flea-circus owner whose grand-uncle leaves him millions in a last will and testament. Of course, his uncle's corrupt lawyer (John Carradine) and business partners have swindled the old man out of the money—and have had him bumped off.

For odd reasons, it sends Fred Allen on a quest to recover money hidden in an old heirloom chair he has given away. In his travels he meets Jack Benny (playing a vain skinflint named Jack Benny).  He flatters Benny by telling him, based on Jack's radio show jokes, he thought he was a much older man. Benny counters that he will be of voting age next year.

*It's in the Bag* is cynical and sharp, dispatching opening movie credits by Allen as a bunch of names you'd find in a phone book, or hangers-on relatives of the movie's producer. He yearns for the day when movies will dispatch opening credits completely.

It's not a great movie, not even a great comedy, but it is an unusual gemstone that puts a timeless, irreverent, insouciant, iconoclastic spin on dumb-founded American culture. No wonder we were charmed by it.

# Lost on Children

Our antipathy for comic book heroes and comic book movies is well known and documented. So, with some trepidation, we pursued *Deadpool*, listed as an anti-comic book movie with an antihero. Well rest assured, readers, this is a comic book movie.

Ryan Reynolds plays Deadpool as swishier than the cast of *Queer as Folk*. He can throw off one liners faster than Rex Harrison in a Noel Coward play. We doubt that anyone watching this movie even knows who Noel Coward is.

On the other hand, *Deadpool* has more movie parodies than your typical Mel Brooks comedy.

Reynolds is more than a match for his pansexual character, which keeps the viewer interested.

If you are looking for a plot, this film will disappoint you. It is strictly a character study about how science has wronged a man and put him into a funny suit.

Friends tell us that the only true philosophical movies today are in the comic book genre. Heaven help us. If you believe that, you have never seen true drama in reality-based movies. This is not Shakespeare, Prince Hamlet.

Exaggeration and hyperbole in comic books apparently make it easier to see larger issues among the dregs of life. It more likely points out the utter failure of the educational system in liberal arts.

We are off base here. *Deadpool* is highly entertaining, quick paced, filled with smutty talk, noisy car chases, bloody killings, sexual situations, and all done tongue-in-cheek.

This is what passes for witty repartee and screwball comedy in the 21st-century.

# Mel Brooks Takes on Hitchcock

Mel Brooks makes lots of noise in the documentary *Mel Brooks: Make a Noise.*

With his participation through extensive interviews annotating parts of his career, this little film covers the complete oeuvre of Brooks from a gag man with Sid Caesar to his ultimate Broadway conquest with a musical version of *The Producers.*

There are so many milestones of hilarity along the way, you begin to comprehend the impact of this writer who, though not particularly religious, played up his Jewish angle like a dog with a bone.

Along the way you will find explanations of the variations of "Springtime for Hitler," and how it was not well received—at first. You will learn Brooks was an 18-year old soldier in World War II, that he was a mentor and god to Gene Wilder. Wildly peppered with film clips from *Young Frankenstein, High Anxiety, The Producers, Spaceballs*, and others, the laughs keep coming even in retrospect.

Many interviews are vintage because the actors and personalities are no longer alive, but Brooks is more than alive. He is energetic, sharp, and full of himself—and what more could you expect?

In one anecdote, he reveals that he had a private showing of *High Anxiety* for Alfred Hitchcock. The film was a send-up and homage to the Master of Suspense. After the shower scene, Hitch turned to Brooks and said, "Absolutely brilliant, but you used 13 shower curtain rings and I used only ten."

If you ever laughed at a Mel Brooks movie, you will love this ultimate compendium from the Master himself.

## Movie Psychos

You could call it a shaggy dog story, but the movie is not a dog at all. We found it one of the most strikingly original movies from a major studio that we have seen.

All your favorite movie bad guys have lined up to lend a bit of the psycho ear, eyes, and nose to this warped comedy.

*Seven Psychopaths* outdoes one *Psycho* with the humor Hitchcock intended for his first psycho. This tale centers around a film writer (Colin Farrell) whose best friend Billy Bickle of the Travis Bickle family (Sam Rockwell). Farrell is writing a movie titled *Seven Psychopaths*, and their collaborative insider tales make up some of the story.

Of course, the term appropriate to the killers is sociopathic, not psychopathic, but who's slicing, dicing and parsing words in this movie?

The real lynchpin of the movie is an adorable *shih tzu* owned by a psycho mobster (Woody Harrelson, of course) who goes berserk when the little doggy is dognapped. Billy Bickle and his collaborator (Christopher Walken) kidnap dogs of the rich and famous and return them several days later for large rewards.

This time the cute dog is the love of Harrelson's life—and it's *mano-a-mano* psychopath warfare when a real life serial killer of serial killers joins the mix to stir up the blood and guts.

The violence is clever and horrifyingly amusing with cameos by some notable actors as victims and perps.

We generally avoid movies about writers having writer's block, but love movies about Hollywood's behind-the-scenes shenanigans. In this stew, director (Martin McDonagh) puts the ingredients into a large crockpot and lets simmer.

## Yes, a Comedy Tonight Literally!

*Mythic Comic Competition: Zero & Phil Silvers*

 Notable composer and writer Stephen Sondheim has always been of two worlds: his high-falutin' musicals, and his low-brow musicals.  He started out writing *Topper* for TV about ghosts in a sit-com—and he wound up as one of the most celebrated of American Broadway composers of *A Little Night Music* and *Sunday in the Park with George.*

We prefer low-brow this time.

We took a look again, years later, of his 1966 low-brow story: *A Funny Thing Happened on the Way to the Forum.* Those who saw it on Broadway are a dying breed, thank heavens, because they always complained the stage version was longer, contained better songs, and was a work of genius.

The movie was directed by Richard Lester in a style that won converts after *A Hard Day's Night.* His frenetic pace and visual burlesque moments are right out of slapstick in ancient Rome.

However, the film is monumental because Zero Mostel recreated his stage performance. Well, it is not exactly a performance. Mostel chews up scenery and  mugs in such a way that defies anything resembling acting. This is a happening. It is beyond, way beyond, perhaps the Twilight Zone goes to the Forum. He is matched by Sgt. Bilko, Phil Silvers in an equally stunning screen travesty.

They are marvelous and will certainly dismiss anyone thinking this could have occurred on Broadway. Throw in Jack Gilford and Patricia Jessel as the shrew harridan of all-time, and Michael Herndon's seminal browbeat husband grows all the more impressive.

The four stars dance along the aqueduct. Buster Keaton only shows up for cameos and the surprise ending.

The leering sexuality is of another age, but that is burlesque, friends.

If ever Broadway musicals were to be staged with perfect segues between action and music, this film accomplishes it.

We recalled it was a show and a half, but it has lost nothing and gained mythic proportions. If you have never seen it, you must stream it now. A comedy tonight indeed.

## Mad Money

***Keaton and Latifah Go Mad!***

We missed *Mad Money* the first time around, and its philosophy and premise as a comedy requires some thought on the part of the audience. That is rather unusual, but we came to an unpleasant conclusion.

The film really stars Diane Keaton and Ted Danson as a late middle-aged couple who bankruptcy occurs when high-pay ends. They are left with a quarter of a million dollars of debt. Housewife Keaton must return to the employment line to help win some bread.

She ends up at the Federal Reserve as a cleaning woman. It seems unlikely that a woman with a degree in Comparative Lit would do this, but she needed the benefits.

Once there, seeing money destroyed, shredded and destroyed by the Feds, she is moved to commit a criminal conspiracy. There is something disturbing that lifelong honest people will be driven to do dastardly criminal activity to survive. It may be true, though none of the honest people we have encountered would do this.

Queen Latifah is also tempted by the concept that crime is a virus and once exposed, you will turn criminal. Even more appalling, honest people are the best kind of criminal because their native intelligence and honesty makes them a head above normal criminal imbeciles.

We had some trouble with these concepts, and it had a distinct effect on our laugh quotient. It became most unfunny to watch this caper film with a gang of unlikely ladies.

It may be a film for fans of Latifah or Keaton, but you must be dyed I the wool to put up with this kind of loose ethical standard.

# No Salad Eating Chick

*Queen & Commoner*

We may be catching this about ten years too late, but better late! Hundreds of views on Amazon Prime say how much they love this movie. Queen Latifah is perfect, not *Just Wright.*

As one of the few oversized women in starring roles, unabashed, she steals every scene with her genuine sweetness in the face of life's adversities.

She plays a physical therapist who has a chance encounter with an NBA star (Common). From there, the breaks seem to go every which way. Phylicia Rashaad plays Common's mother, and Pam Grier plays Latifah's mother. We have something going on here.

We were mostly bowled over and amused to find another Boston icon in the movie: Latifah starred with Tom Brady's wife in one picture, and here in all the basketball scenes is former Celtic, Rajon Rondo.

This romantic comedy with a basketball setting has all the wrong turns and twists of fate you might expect that throw the crossed paths of Latifah and Common back together repeatedly.

Because Queen Latifah is not your standard trophy wife of a pro athlete type, this film takes on more gravitas. Common is a tad short for the NBA but is likeable and good-looking. But Rondo is a better actor, but Dwight Howard has a bigger scene.

The inevitable twist of fate brings the physical therapist into physical contact with the superstar in contract negotiations, and the big pay-off must satisfy the audience.

This is sheer fantasy, as any fan can tell you. Players are never thrown into a big game full-time after a career injury, but spend weeks acclimating. But this is a movie romance.

Queen Latifah even hums a few bars from "The More I See You," in one scene as a throwaway to her old musical career. She's billed as musical consultant. Don't be fooled: this is still a jazzy gem.

## Unexpected Slapstick

*Laughton & Costello!*

Almost ten years after his low-budget pirate on the bounding sea as *Captain Kidd* and 20 years after Bligh's *Mutiny on the Bounty*, Charles Laughton jumped at the chance to reprise Captain Kidd. He had also the opportunity to reprise Henry VIII in a movie with Bette Davis as his daughter, Queen Elizabeth. They famously greeted each other as "Father," and "Daughter," off screen too.

Now, the irascible Laughton would poke fun at himself and his performance as Captain Kidd confronting scene-stealer emeritus Lou Costello. Perhaps that was the true challenge for Laughton and his Oscar-level talent. He was about to show he could play vaudeville with the best of them.

*Abbott & Costello Meet Captain Kidd* was another in a long series of features in which the comic duo came across monsters of cinema, historical figures, and pratfalls of comedy.

Dignity knows nothing of being a performer with an audience eating out of their backhand of talent. Laughton was a comedian at heart and could steal a scene before Costello could roll an eye.

We were surprised at how many pratfalls Lou Costello gave. Any barrel he hid within was blown up. The big surprise was Laughton: he took the falls without a stuntman. Chairs were pulled out from under him and he plopped onto the floor, and he fell face first into sand in another. It was noteworthy.

If ever there was something unseemly, it was that this comic version of 1953 was in Technicolor, which was never the case for the earlier Laughton masterpieces. If there was a silver lining on the silver screen of the 1950s, it was that garish color fit the bill. There were plenty of explosions among the song and dance routines.

If ever there was a chance to make a side-trip to Oak Island and bury a treasure, this little pirate satire gave us a vision of outright lunacy. A map in the opening credits could be Oak Island.

You start off with a musical introduction to Laughton as the crew sings and dances on their ship, and Kidd sneers at the mention of women. Yup, Laughton had to love this.

We were mostly appalled.

## Elementary, School That is.

We were warned, and now you are warned.

The Will Ferrell and John C. Reilly remake of a comic Conan Doyle couple is not exactly a blue-plate special. It is going for .99 cents on Amazon streaming video. You know that price is rock bottom for rock bottom quality. This is a step down for the Step Brothers.

The film is horrific in terms of anachronisms. There are references to killer bees, protein shakes, and headlines that smell of National Enquirer in the 1950s.

Worse yet are the fake British accents on our traditional heroes, showing that they cherish good acting as much as a paycheck. The actors playing them as children speak with American accents (as do all the kids in London).

Mrs. Hudson is a trollop—and not from the British pages of classic literature.

We almost expected Judi Dench was likely offered the role as Queen Victoria—and that would have set us off on a tangent. Instead, we have Ralph Fiennes acting in a separate movie as Moriarty.

He has no flair for comedy.

Perhaps the most surprising couple in the film are the Road Trip movie stars: Rob Brydon as Lestrade and Steve Coogan as the one-armed tattooist.

We almost wish they had played Holmes and Watson. Of course, this may be the only version in which Lestrade is smarter than Holmes.

The movie moribundly moves from one witless encounter and set-up to another. Killer bees are inexplicably in a glass case at 221b Baker Street, allowing for a madcap moment without suspense.

Another stupid setup is Holmes surprise birthday party thrown by the Queen.  Who wrote this drivel? Mindless is the *Zeitgeist* of the age: and if this is you, you will be in your element.

Yes, it's elementary.  Elementary school.

## Bittersweet Docdrama Dramedy

The resemblance to Laurel and Hardy is uncanny.

*Stan & Ollie* has a resurrection quality to its stars.

You might credit makeup masters, but there is also the subtle posture and gesture of the two stars as they mimic the familiar comedic personalities of the great movie team of the 1930s.

You have likely seen these two stars doing star turns in popular movies with tepid reviews: this is their best work and may end up being their least viewed movie. Laurel and Hardy belong to aficionados of film. Young people (meaning anyone under 40—or even 50—may be in the dark about the great comic duo).

John C. Reilly plays Babe Hardy, Mr. Oliver Hardy to you. And Steve Coogan plays Stan Laurel. A Brit and a Southern gentleman were an unlikely partnership but were created by studio chemists. It was a team that clicked so well it became legend.

The movie starts in 1937 at their pinnacle of success, doing *Way Out West* and their amazing little dance routine. It is repeated several times for good measure. Badly paid, with little artistic credit, Stan Laurel feels slighted as Chaplin and even Buster Keaton received more accolades.

By 1953, on the down-slide with age and television co-opting their earlier films, they embark on a tour of the British Isles to re-kindle their magic. Alas, the movie turns bittersweet, with far more bitter than sweet. Breaking up is never easy.

Bad blood, old age, and festering antagonisms, seem to dog the two stars. The movie replays their famous routines as if it is part of their real lives. And, they are pure show busy folks: the show must go on, and they are always on. Poor, dear souls.

Fans may find this hard look harder to take than a Hal Roach (Danny Huston) cheapskate contract. As oldsters, they had to work; no fortune followed fame.

Younger viewers may well be advised to go back to movies like *Way Out West,* or shorts like *Their First Mistake,* for seeing comedy genesis. This movie, like old age itself, is anticlimactic.

## Over-rated Classic

*Ate for Dinner .*

Your first reaction to this chestnut of horror comedy is shock at the jaw-dropping cast.

Boris Karloff, Charles Laughton, Melvyn Douglas, Raymond Massey, Gloria Stuart, and Ernest Thesiger!  You have a round-robin of possible villains and victims. The problem is that they are given nothing significant to perform. Even

Karloff uses makeup to look menacing, but his dumb waiter is left hanging.

Yeah, it was a dark and stormy night, but that ain't enough.

James Whale gathered quite a retinue of talent and gave them an empty script in a drafty house.

Billed as an atmospheric thriller comedy, that's about all this J.B. Priestly story is. With a marvelous cast, and Whale's shadows and tricks, like a fun house mirror, the plot is ridiculous, throwing a bunch of ingrates caught in a bad torrential rain into a private household as if it's a flea-bag hotel. T'aint funny.

Here they find their hosts eccentric (well, Horace Femm is Ernest Thesiger, which says it all) and his odd-ball bully sister.

Charles Laughter as Sir William shows up too with a show biz girlfriend, and he is given little to do. Melvyn Douglas is his trademark self, complete with pipe, and Boris Karloff still is given no dialogue yet again in one of his movies. He just looks menacing as Morgan, the scar-faced butler.

We wanted so much for this film to give us a thrill and become a marvel, but we found it disappointing to the ultimate degree—and in no way does it hold up to the other horror tales of the Universal series. This alleged classic is a let-down from the get-go.

## Cary Grant & Reel History

*Cary & Randy.*

Let's dig into the vault of RKO movies from 1940 and pull out a plum. Yep, it's Cary Grant and Irene Dunne in *My Favorite Wife,* directed by Garson Kanin.

We presume this was quite the sophisticated, if not racy, comedy of its era. And, it does have a few eyebrow lifting moments!

Grant is a Harvard lawyer whose wife was presumed drowned on a voyage to a South Sea island. He is about to remarry when she shows up with more wackiness than you'd usually find in an *I Love Lucy* episode.

It's all rather slow for the first half of the movie. Actually it only comes to life when Grant discovers that his wife (known as Eve) spent seven years alone on an island with her Adam. It turns out that Adam is acrobatic hunk Randolph Scott.

Rumors about the two stars were in high fettle even back in those days—and the interplay between them is priceless. If you like in-jokes, this one lets everyone in on it. A passerby finds Grant ogling Randy and mopping his brow in distress when a middle-aged woman asks him if that is Johnny Tarzan Weissmuller.

Grant notes he wishes he were.

Once again Cary is caught modeling women's clothing by a psychiatrist with a knowing smile. It's all a great misunderstanding, of course. It's Enoch Arden by ways of Shakespeare and writer Leo McCarey.

As sophisticated comedy, this has more subtext than anyone ever suspected. It may not be a great Grant film, but it belongs in the canon, but the powder puff is never quite dry as screwball comedy or comedy of manners.

# So-so Soviet

***Khrushchev & Malenkov at Stalin's funeral.***

Maybe we missed the lesson of the Cold War in which the ruthless homicidal dictator killer was surrounded by fawning idiots like extras and *operetta* buffoons. *The Death of Stalin* makes a point that defies historical truth.

Indeed, the opening minutes may strike you as a *Monty Python*-style farce (compounded with the appearance of Michael Palin), with a posse of dunces dancing to the whim of Stalin. They must entertain him and do his bidding, lest they end up like everyone else:  on a hit list.

Their cruel inaction over the dying Stalin as he lay on the floor in his *odeur* is the nastiest of political satire. Jeffrey Tambor is Malenkov, the weaking second-in-command and under heavy pressure from Khrushchev (Buschemi).

The film features endless background executions in a variety of appalling ways, carried out ruthlessly, to the gallows humor of men like Nikita Khrushchev, played in thin fashion by Steve Buschemi.

Most of the Communist comrades speak with British accents, jarring at first, ridiculous in deliberance.

What starts as a black comedy set in 1953 becomes more and more disturbing, despite pathetic Vasily Stalin and sister Svetlana, horrified and fearful at what might befall them with their despot father's death.

From the early antics of a *Monty Python*, the film devolves into *The Godfather*, as these small-minded committee commies become more frightful and violent. We can almost fully believe there is more political truth than satire here. This is Swiftian justice meted out by the Lilliputians.

The evolution of Nikita Khrushchev from second banana to dangerous rival to the predatory Beria, Stalin's child molesting henchman, is truly the centerpiece of this political free-for-all. Buschemi's performance is ultimately a marvel to behold.

Fast-moving and surprising, it is a film to put on your viewing list.

# Reincarnation Mystery Turns the Screw

***Kookoo Noir Takeoff***

There was a time nearly 30 years ago when Kenneth Branagh was considered the reincarnation of Orson Welles, with a dollop of Laurence Olivier thrown into the mix.

So, the time has arrived to re-assess one of his early efforts called *Dead Again* from 1991.

He was a promising and brilliant director of unusual fare and acted well too. This looney mystery deviated from his usual Shakespearean play adaptations by entering the *film noir*, detective story, broadly copying Warner and Paramount features of the late 1940s.

What most missed back then was the fact that this overwrought tale of reincarnation and murder was overdone deliberately. We cannot believe Branagh was dumb enough to think this was not a comedy.

The film does double duty: telling a modern case of a detective Mike Church in LA today, and the strange killer, Roman Strauss, a composer and conductor of 1948, who was executed for murdering his wife. The black and white *noir* flashbacks are spot on for 1940s imitation. Dick Powell and Lizabeth Scott are suitably channeled.

Branagh is a little weird as a detective (his reincarnated self) who is an LA sleuth with a Brooklyn accent. That might be the first mistake, or first clue.

The cast is equally impressive, with Emma Thompson as Strauss's wife, the concert pianist victim, and the modern woman with amnesia that Church must help.

Call in Derek Jacobi as some kind of psychic hypnotist to regress the woman to 1948, and you have another brilliant performer slightly out of place in an American movie.

Also hanging around in cameos are Robin Williams, Scott Campbell, and Andy Garcia. This film is no slouch when it comes to top-level talent. Yes, Wayne Knight is here too.

We are a sucker when it comes to transgender resurrection and timeless love stories.

Everyone immediately notices that Emma Thompson resembles a woman dead in 1948, but no one seems to notice that Kenneth Branagh resembles her convicted murderer, executed in 1949.

Oh, well, that's *Life Magazine* for you. In the meantime, the movie moves more and more toward utter lunacy, skipping over plot holes like hopscotch gone to bad karma.

We like our twist of reincarnation with a bitter of gender bending. Add some lemons and you have Branagh imitating Paramount and Warner Brothers murder mystery thrillers of the 1940s with panache. We are *Between Two Worlds* and *the Two Mrs. Carrolls*.

Like a warm British beer, this movie is all frothy, and the suds will make you queasy. It's eye-rolling fun.

## Original Stars, 30 Years Later

*Grumpiness as a Joy to Behold!*

The two men who single-handedly created a movie/TV franchise of Neil Simon's comedy classic stageplay, Jack Lemmon and Walter Matthau, returned twenty years ago, aged in the wood, to reprise their roles as Oscar and Felix.

We discovered *Odd Couple 2* to cheer us so many years later.

We confess to having missed this event when it happened, and we were surprised to find it available now on streaming format. It is, however, a sad and bittersweet experience to behold. The two great stars keep their chemistry, but age has sapped them of vitality. It is like watching Laurel and Hardy in their final film.

Time is never kind.

Oscar and Felix have been separated for nearly twenty years, though they made the original film in the late 1960s, and the sequel is 30 years later. They are brought together by the marriage of Felix's daughter to Oscar's son.

Jokes about slobs and neatniks have been replaced with a series of old age jabs and dollops of humor.

More than ever these grumpy old men (Lemmon & Matthau) epitomize Oscar and Felix, as if the aging process has turned them into fine wine.

The storyline is filled with pratfalls and lowbrow situations as the two men battle each other's foibles in the California desert, trying to make it to a wedding.

Though the situation is forced, you must see past that and simply enjoy the actors as they return to their beloved characters, not missing a beat, not letting age and time distract their timing and their experience.

## Second Bananas are Tops

A major star before Shirley Temple was born, Rose Marie's last act was the receive the lifetime Shirley Temple Award in 2017. *Waiting for Your Laugh* is her testimonial, made with her cooperation shortly before she died in 2017.

Never a beauty, but always a beaut. As a child, Rose Marie counted among her friends and supporters, gangsters like Al Capone and Bugsy Siegel.  Capone told her to call him "Uncle Al."

She helped Bugsy build a resort entertainment venue that happened to be Las Vegas. She was the first headline and didn't think twice to tell Siegel her paycheck was short $11.

He apologized and paid up.

She worked with them all—from Jimmy Durante to Milton Berle. Among her friends were Jerry Lewis and Johnny Carson, whom she called "angels." They all treated her like a daughter and she liked all of them.

She learned how to do standup comedy to enhance her singing career. And, when TV demanded, she became a character actress on shows like *Gunsmoke.* Though she performed movies and Broadway, nightclubs were her secret passion. She played everywhere in America.

When TV comedy needed her, she did the Dick Van Dyke Show when no one knew who he was. She did a dozen years on Hollywood Squares, and made dozens of guest shots as cranky old bossy women. Her coworkers like Morey Amsterdam and Peter Marshall adored her.

In a time when old singers were forgotten, she organized Rosemary Clooney, Margaret Whiting, and Helen O'Connell, into a lucrative concert series.

Rose Marie lived 90 years, a staple of entertainment for multiple generations and only passed away last year.

In her love life, there was the greatest tragedy, having found the ideal man, Bobby Guy, a trumpeter from Kay Keyser and Bing Crosby bands, but who died too young—stealing her only personal love besides work.

This compelling documentary cannot be stopped. It unfolds and hypnotizes like Rose Marie herself.

## British or Black?

*Dinklage with Friend in Coffin*

In case you did not realize, there are two versions of this movie, made within a few years of each other. The first was your classic British dark comedy, and the second is your black-face remake in American ghetto mode.

Both movies are called *Death at a Funeral,* which certainly makes sense when you see how it all plays out. The Brit version is from 2007, and the American from 2010.

You can flip a coin, or perhaps you prefer Ivory-Merchant to Medea.

We went across the pond for ours. There are familiar faces, but we'd probably know more of the cast in the American version. However, one small face stands out in a big part: Peter Dinklage came up to snuff in both films as the blackmailing small guy.

He is rather good, for sure. The rest of the cast is obtuse, but we must confess that Rupert Graves is always a joy as the successful brother returning from America for his father's sendoff.

We are not sure how funny the central concept is that some poor benighted fools are given LSD by accident by those who think they offer valium. Is that really funny?

Beyond that, there are some jokes about oldsters, women, and sex-starved creeps among the mourners. It's all directed by Frank Oz, hardly anyone's idea of Ivory-Merchant, unless you see in big screen Muppet. Peter Dinklage apparently is playing Kermit in this film—and in the other too. He is marvelous.

We aren't sure how this comes off with Chris Rock, *et al*, when the British posh types seem more suited for deadpan comedy.

## Art Buchwald Satire with Sir Noel

### *Mitzi & Noël sing and dance!*

Sir Noël, showman and epitome of the English gentleman, made a plethora of movies from the late 1950s to the late 1960s. He only turned down playing *Dr. No* in the James Bond spy movie.

From *Our Man in Havana* to *the Italian Job,* he lent his delectable presence in costarring roles. In 1960 he went opposite Yul Brynner in the Stanley Donen comedy called *Surprise Package.*

The big surprise is that it was written by satirist Art Buchwald, though you would never know it. Our favorite humorist seems lost in this adapted script.

Apart from the delicious scenes between mobster Nico March (Yul) and the deposed and exiled King Pavel the Patient (Noël), the movie is not really funny or smart. However, every time you find Brynner and Coward in matchup mode, there is something extraordinary going on.

You almost have the sense that the film was meant for someone else: perhaps James Cagney, to shoot dialogue like a machine gun. Mitzi Gaynor seems to be playing Judy Holiday. Brynner is on top of it, impressive as always.

No one else in movies could have played the deadpan, throwaway lines like Noël Coward. He's in his own movie world, like Mae West. The rest of the cast is along for the ride.

Coward steals every moment on camera, like the master showman he always was. He could depose Burton and Taylor in *Boom*, and so going up against Yul Brynner shortly before *the Magnificent Seven* might have amused Noël.

It's a soufflé, for sure, and perhaps the success of Donen brought Coward in for the Greek isle locations shooting.

Yul had just finished another comedy with Donen, and likely enjoyed the change of pace from epical heroes and villains.

*Surprise Package* would be a bad TV movie nowadays with execrable actors. However, when the legends at the top of their game deign to appear in silly roles, you must pay attention.

# Sir Noël Always Busy

***Caine & Coward Comedy!***

Noël Coward and Benny Hill? In the same movie?

Our attention has been caught big-time in this 1969 crime caper movie, a *genre* all the rage in the 1960s, with epitome *The Italian Job.* Forget the recent remake.

As if pairing those Benny and Noël was enough, you add in Rossano Brazzi and Raf Vallone as the genuine Italians—and Michael Caine as the British mastermind of a robbery in Turin, Italy, of gold bullion being driven through its narrow streets.

The film is lusciously produced with all those magnificent scenes of the historic Italian city and the gorgeous Italian Alps with its twisty roads. You can figure on car chases that will outdo all those hills in San Francisco.

As with classics like this, the actual production is less impressive. The stars seem self-contained in their roles. Indeed, there are no scenes with Brazzi and his fellow stars at all. The closest Benny Hill comes to Noël Coward is standing 50 feet away on a mole hill at a funeral.

The glue is a boyish and charming Michael Caine, so young that when he meets Noël Coward in a lavatory, you almost feel it is salacious.

Waspy Coward is a mob kingpin, believe it or don't, who has bribed enough people to move in and out of his British prison cell with aplomb you'd expect from a sophisticated star. He runs everything with an iron fist in a dainty velvet glove.

Technology, alas, is ancient here. Good heavens, Benny Hill plays a computer nerd running around with a ten-inch reel of programming. Communication is also primitive with 16mm film as the preferred mode to send text messages. Yet, the charm is delightful and timeless.

Once the cars start piling up, you have a traffic jam for the pre-Euro-dollar ages.

## Cary Grant Finale

*Bad, Not Good*

After watching the inimitable Cary Grant's life in his own words in a brilliant documentary, it was time to look at his last film performance, one we had missed all these years.

In 1966, silver-haired and dapper, looking no different than he had for a decade, Cary was growing disenchanted with playing a leading man opposite young women, much younger women.

So, he took a page out of an old co-star's catalogue of film roles. In *Monkey Business,* he worked with oldster Charles

Coburn, who played for two decades the curmudgeon old man to great delight.

Grant found a film script for *The More the Merrier* that Coburn had brought to the screen in the mid-1940s. It was about an old reprobate who was forced to share an apartment with a girl young enough to be his grand-daughter because of a housing shortage.

Update twenty years later, and Cary played a British baronet in Tokyo for the Olympics too early and without a place to stay. For reasons ridiculous, he ends ups forcing his way into beautiful Samantha Eggar's small flat.

If living with 'gramps' was meant to be full of generational embarrassments, this film misfired badly. It was not gramps, but attractive and youthful Cary Grant. He was no Charles Coburn. Try as he might, Cary could not pull off a curmudgeon, only a curdled performance.

It is disappointing and pathetic—and perhaps gave him full convincing that it was time to walk away from movies.

Hitchcock tried to give him a few good roles in the 1960s, but Cary was done with appearing as the star, either in comedy or drama.

It's a sad state to see a great star floundering with his wonderful manner in a bad script, miscast, and poorly directed.

Run as fast as you can from *Walk, Don't Run*. It's terrible.

## Mad Director Meets Madder Stunt Man

If you ever wondered what it might've been like to walk onto the set of legendary superstar Peter O'Toole during filming, your chance came in 1980 with the movie *The Stunt Man*, directed by Richard Rush.

The title is two words because Burt Reynolds sued director Rush over the title, wanting it for his movie tribute to stuntmen. They split the difference.

It's a comedy action thriller drama Hollywood insider movie about the making of an out-of-control World War I epic anti-war movie with more explosions and killings than supports its so-called plot of the movie-within-a-movie.

It also costars Steve Railsback, in a rare heroic role as a Vietnam vet with post-traumatic stress syndrome. Fleeing from police, he wanders onto the set of O'Toole's Eli Cross production and is immediately sucked into the ruse of taking up the role of a stunt man who was killed accidentally that day.

O'Toole knows he has a fugitive on his hands, but needs to prevent an investigation into his botched movie stunt.

Railsback was fresh off playing Charles Manson in *Helter-Skelter* for a movie mini-series. Peter O'Toole based his wacky director on his work with David Lean during the making of *Lawrence of Arabia.*

Flying around the set on a crane, O'Toole's ego-maniacal director will risk anything to get his movie on film, including the accidental death of crew-members. Yes, this is a comedy, but not quite like you expect.

This movie probably would never be made today, even with rogue directors and winking cable studios financing the project.  Then, again, we admit that *Twin Peaks* was given a green-light.

When Railsback asks O'Toole why he is protecting the fugitive, O'Toole answers: "Because I'm in love with your dark side." It makes perfect sense.

Railsback was never so handsome, and O'Toole was never quite so cuckoo.  It makes for a delicious movie, though it is about a half-hour too long.

In its earlier incarnation, it was given little publicity in its release. O'Toole commented the film was not released, "It escaped."

## Nearest Thing to Heaven

You cannot judge *An Affair to Remember* by any normal standard of film-making. Since its 1957 debut, Leo McCarey's dinosaur storyline and archaic approach passes for classic movie-making.

The film has anachronisms abounding, but cast that aside. It is the cast he assembled and has given them reins of control. Cary Grant and Deborah Kerr are at the peak of their careers, slightly past the middle-age that would soon have them by-passed by a new Hollywood.

The film's plot is a trifle, yet elegant, charming, sophisticated, and sentimental. Your stars are clearly not typical American celebrities, and they play social climbers way ahead of their social standing, ready to plunge into high society by means of deceptive façade. Any fault in this movie does not lie in the stars.

On a ship voyage to the United States, Cary and Deborah have a frothy, light comedy of interplay, under the watchful eye of paparazzi and gossip. It's a pink champagne tale. Engaged to money, they both eschew this for true love before it's too late.

Interspersed here is a small role by Cathleen Nesbitt as Cary's grandmother. She's closer to the age of his real mother, but no matter. The trio of actors know something about loss: Nesbitt in her youth was engaged to marry the beautiful poet Rupert Brooke when he was killed in World War I. Grant went through multiple marriages and gave up Randy Scott.

Add a melody that remains an emotional stake in the heart, replayed constantly to put tragedy next to love. It isn't a mid-life Tristan and Isolde, but it will do.

The film may cause you to weep through a box of Kleenex. If not, you are a victim of Medusa's stony glare. You cannot watch the final 15 minutes of the film and not find two actors in better form anywhere.

## Movie Myths in Song & Dance

You may remember *La La Land* as the film that won the Oscar for five minutes. It was a mistake, for sure. We aren't sure if the film is supposed to be a take-off, or a throwback, or just to feel good old-fashioned musical. It may be much more.

*La la Land* is some mystic, mythic American place where gridlock results in a mile-long sing-along.  If this is your cup of tea, stay out of Starbucks. If you love movies, this has more movie references than a Mel Brooks comedy. Yet, this one is a romantic gem.

Director Damien Chazelle manages to squeeze everything from Fellini's *8 & a Half* to *Rebel without a Cause* into his film, while resonating Gene Kelly's *American in Paris.*

Ryan Gosling's character wants to single-handedly save jazz for a new generation—and Chazelle does too. We thought there must be a trick to Gosling's piano performance, which is bravura at the least. He sings and dances too.

Emma Stone's eyes may be reminiscent of Bette Davis, but she is show busy to the *nth* degree. Attention, movie fans, we have a movie here, right down to the fluorescent green drapes out of *Vertigo.*

Dreams in *La-La Land* may be achievable—but at great cost, though the journey is richly detailed in this hypnotic movie.

The last musical we enjoyed was *A Chorus Line,* which we saw a dozen times because our friend Jimmy Kirkwood wrote it. He loved show biz stories too, and this would have grabbed him.

Though this movie missed out on its big Oscar, it's the sort that will live in legend and re-telling and re-viewing in the generations to come. You cannot miss this film and call yourself a fan of Hollywood, jazz, or creative impulse.

# Early Bewitched

After Hitchcock made them a romantic couple with perfect chemistry in *Vertigo*, they made another film that year. It was called *Bell, Book, & Candle.*

It was a sharp satire about a coven of witness in Manhattan.

James Stewart and Kim Novak excelled in turning suspense to laughs, with an assist from actors like Jack Lemmon and Ernie Kovacs.

At least one scene echoes Novak's San Francisco apartment in Vertigo, but she has a scene-stealing cat named Piwacket this time.

Stewart is a book publisher who falls under Novak's spell, but the entire concept was done to death in the 1960s under the TV series name of *Bewitched*. The original idea here seems to have been undercut over the years—except for the striking adult subtlety.

Lemmon and Kovacs shack up in a hotel room to write a book, but their relationship sounds a great deal like consenting adults. They play it to the hilt in the closeted 1950s, which may be the biggest surprise. The Zodiac Club where Lemmon hangs out with other warlocks certainly doubles for a 1950s gay club.

Novak is stunningly beautiful, and Stewart still has enough in the tank to be at the top of his game. The scenes shot in New York with body doubles indicate that Stewart and Novak never left the Hollywood studio when making this film.

The magic of movies is perfect here, from the lush color, muted effects of witchcraft, and the interplay of adults not into situation comedy.

# Pride Before the Fall

Jane Austen likely would feel violated by *Pride and Prejudice and Zombies.* When you're dead, they stomp all over you.

Just exactly who is the audience of this trifle? Austen's deft comedy of manners has been lightly dusted with the walking dead. It is not an idea to warm the cockles of Austen fans, and it is far too genteel for a zombie aficionado.

So, what's the point? Is it to enhance Austen to introduce her to a new audience of readers? We suspect zombie fans don't read anything but graphic novels.

The changes are odd too. It seems the lovely sisters of Austen's book have been sent to China to learn how to be Ninjas. Oh, really? China in early 19th century was a haven for women's lib? Perhaps once they unbound their feet, young girls might take charge.

The movie is high gloss and well-produced. Period films are not easy to create, and much effort was put into the manners, mores, and cultural artifacts of England in 1810.

When a comedy of manners becomes a farce of horror, you may want to call on Mary Shelley. We believe firmly that Jane Austen never felt the need to compete with the gothic horrors of Shelley, or even those other sisters, the Brontes.

It's doubtful we'll soon see a spate of films on the lines of *Abe Lincoln: Vampire Hunter* or *Sherlock Holmes and the Sign of the Four Zombies*, but we shall not bet against it.

## Sgt. Bilko Meets Lawrence of Arabia!

Call us astonished when we discovered that there is a movie wherein Sergeant Ernest T. Bilko meets *Beau Geste* and lands us in an oasis of British comedy about the French Foreign Legion.

Well, it's something akin to that. It seems when Phil Silvers had his famous Bilko TV series cancelled, he went off to merry old England and made a movie with the *Carry On…* gang. It was called *Follow That Camel* and was made in 1967.

In beautiful Technicolor, Silvers shines with his usual schtick. He plays Sgt. Nocker of the French Foreign Legion in 1906. For all purposes, he is Bilko, barking orders the same way he did in his hit show *You'll Never Get Rich*.

Oh, his commandant is a German right out of *Stalag 17*, and there are more belly dancers than you could possibly imagine for Silvers to leer at in the Zig Zag Cafe.

If there was a big difference between the Bilko show and the movie version, it was simply that sexual innuendo was given a free hand. Of course, by today's standards, Mae West is safe for children. So is Phil Silvers as he sticks his nose into bosoms.

When you dig down deep, there is nothing much to this film except the fun of seeing Phil Silvers continue his personification of a wheeling and dealing con man. He is obsequious to superiors and a shark to others, all hilariously done.

Since *Follow That Camel* never had a wide distribution to American theaters, we had to find it by accident on Amazon Instant for a nominal fee. Yes, we did feel Bilko had fleeced us by the end of the 90 minutes, but we loved every penny spent.

## As Funny as a Migraine

We love Westerns, and we are horrified by something called *A Million Ways to Die in the West*. If writer/producer/director/star Seth McFarlane thinks he is any of the above, we beg to differ. This is not Orson Welles making a movie; it is not even Woody Allen doing a parody.

An alleged comedy/satire/burlesque/parody, this stinkeroo may be considered a misfire by a Gatling gun.

This film tries to juxtapose modern parlance of the main character Albert with everyone else in Western veneer. Filled with witless profanity and ugly sexual references, the humor must be knocking them dead if audiences are high on dope.

A big budget, high gloss film, the movie has elements of music that reminds one the big westerns of the 1950s. Scenery and plot holes are right out of the heyday of oaters. We almost wish this had been toned down to a reasonable bad movie. Instead, this film is a colossal misstep, working hard to do pratfalls.

Oh, a few performers always shine no matter how deep in sheep dip their movie paycheck can be found. Neil Patrick Harris and Liam Neeson actually rise above the material, though it would only take one step up on the step-ladder to achieve this height.

One heavy stepping dance sequence makes us yearn for *Seven Brides for Seven Brothers,* but instead we have flatulence jokes that *Blazing Saddles* wore out forty years ago.

The concept of the picture seems to be that the West was a dangerous place filled with menace and sickness. Most of that is in the mind of Seth McFarlane who has seen enough Westerns to miss their point.

Taking most set-ups in western movies, this story goes from one gag to another, making foul language and brutality the stuff of humor.

We rate this movie: "Just Awful."

## Missing Peter O'Toole

Some thirty years ago we first watched Peter O'Toole in *My Favorite Year*. He was resoundingly praised for his portrayal of a combination of himself and Errol Flynn.

The plot was allegedly based on the old Sid Caesar show when Flynn was guest star. We doubt it.

O'Toole was in a separate movie than the rest of the cast as Alan Swann. We have been mesmerized by these star vehicles many times. Perhaps the majesty of the star renders everyone else to look like extras on TV commercial in 1954.

Directed by Richard Benjamin like a TV pilot episode of Dick Van Dyke's comedy writers, there was a flavor of 1954 in scenes. Was this the Golden Age of television in reality? It's doubtful.

Playing himself as a younger star in film clips, sword fighting and kissing damsels, O'Toole is marvelous. He was Lawrence of Arabia and Lord Jim, Henry II young and old.

So, to see him play homage to old Errol was a treat. Unfortunately, we had to put up with a nebbish hero sidekick in Mark Linn-Baker. Where did he go? Based on this movie, not far enough. He was not engaging or charming, but a thorn under the saddle.

Out on the town, adored by crowds, O'Toole's swashbuckler takes it in stride. It was a bit of comeback for the great star— much like Barrymore and Flynn came back as shadow satires of their younger selves.

O'Toole died in 2013, making only a few rare film appearances in the later years. Nothing could match his early grandeur—and this was the last of those efforts.

We waited for every scene with O'Toole, claiming he was not an actor! He was a movie star! Oh, yes, make that Movie Star! And what an actor!!

## Original and Best

If you want timeless classics, you cannot find anything remotely close to a rare David Lean directed comedy, written and produced by Noel Coward. The delightful *Blithe Spirit* transcended its time of 1945 with lively repartee and shockingly modern sensibilities.

Novelist Charles Condomine (Rex Harrison) has invited a daffy cliché-ridden medium named Madame Acarti (Margaret Rutherford) to his home to study her for "tricks of the trade" for his new book.

One séance leads to another. Charles's overly minx-like dead first wife named Elvira shows up to complicate his life and present marriage to staid Ruth.

It's one of those ironic British tales where the ultra-rich shut off lights to save electricity, but they dress four times per day for each meal with increasing foppery. Saving the best for last, Rex Harrison and Constance Cummings are dressed to the nines for dinner, just themselves of course. What a quaint era.

As Elvira in ghastly grey and green makeup to make her fade into a faded color movie, Kay Hammond is utterly wonderful as the acerbic Elvira—making off-hand comments on the medium and guests with aplomb.

As Madame Arcati, Margaret Rutherford made an impression on movie audiences, though her big success was still a decade away. The old gal simply steals every moment of film she shares with anyone else in the cast.

That is no mean feat with Rex Harrison in his most classic glib demeanor. It's Henry Higgins with Ruth as Colonel Pickering and Elvira as Eliza. Every moment is a classic, and David Lean deftly shows he could handle even the soufflés that Noel Coward half-baked.

Short, sweet, and with a light touch on special effects, the charm is just right.

## Spirit Network, Pre-Cable

*Natwick, Bacall, Colbert, Hover Over Coward*

With the passing of Lauren Bacall not a few weeks ago, and with the recent live television event of *Peter Pan,* we were moved to a degree of nostalgia.

We went on a scavenger hunt to find one of the few performances by Miss Bacall that we had missed along the way: her live television role as Elvira in *Blithe Spirit,* a 1956 production with Claudette Colbert and Noel Coward, starring and directing his most clever and brilliant light comedy.

Video Collectors of California actually had a black & white edition, rare and seldom seen, but worth every moment. To think that audiences at home decades ago had live television plays with major stars shames today's world of hundreds of cable channels with shoddy repeats.

Colbert and Bacall play the two wives of Charles Condomine, a second-rate writer who wants to do a book on charlatan mediums. Mildred Natwick reprises her 1940s Broadway stage role here as dotty, cliché ridden Madame Acarti.

The result is magical. With special effects done live, and well before computer generated efforts, we have understated and perfectly fitting ghostly shenanigans. You see, Mr. Condomine's first wife (Bacall) is dead—and returns unceremoniously to haunt his second wife (Colbert).

Crossed between the full-blown movie version and stage depictions, the television version is remarkable for its medium range. It has the best of both worlds, spiritual and physical, as well as film and primitive video.

Directed by the author and with his debonair send-up style, Noel Coward provides a delicious concoction. And, the television production is true to the play's ending.

If you want an unusual treat, it would pay to look for this DVD version of the Emmy-winning show from the Golden Age of Television.

Wonderful and wondrous, we enjoyed every second.

# Third Time is No Charm

## *Bogarde & Gordon Blow It Big Time!*

We all know the legendary story of the actor on his deathbed who said, "Dying is easy. Comedy is hard."

To die on live national television is now an actor's lost dream. You can't blow it on live TV when they won't let you work for genuine laughs unless it is stand-up.

There are still ways to prove your mettle as an actor when you are a highly respected movie star. One is to perform live comedy in a play—say the likes of Noel Coward. Now that seems easy. Didn't Rex Harrison throw away lines all the time in Coward style?

We recently watched Noel Coward doing his own *Blithe Spirit* on live television in 1956 (a video copy, old wags). And now, we wanted to see one of our favorite actors Dirk Bogarde give it a shot in 1966.

He seemed right on the surface: British, handsome, pleasant, but deep down his specialty has always been some kind of existential suffering. He should have left that style at the door. It works in *Death in Venice*, not here.

Poor Bogarde. His comedy seems less manners and blacker. Someone must have told him he was doing Edward Albee, not Noel Coward. He shouts at his wife like they are a road show of Burton and Taylor.

He steps on every laugh. Alas, in this Hallmark Hall of Fame production from 1966, so does his costar Ruth Gordon as Madame Acarti. Her singular acting delivery seems not to know where pause meets laugh.

Rachel Roberts actually suffers most here as Ruth because she is on the money around the penny-pinchers of laughs. Rosemary Harris is Elvira in traditional fashion.

Yes, comedy is hard when you die on live TV. Don't go looking for this version of *Blithe Spirit* unless you are into historical tragedy.

## Coburn as Satan

A cheesy porn film with a similar title has done a grave disservice to a chestnut movie way ahead of its time.

*The Devil and Miss Jones* would be called dramedy decades later, but it is a charming romantic comedy film of 1941. It is too often confused with the notorious *The Devil in Miss Jones.* What a shame.

We were stunned by the pairing of crotchety old Charles Coburn as a billionaire without a conscience and a shoe salesgirl in the form of Jean Arthur. It seems the department store chain is having union organizers burning the owner in effigy. Coburn, a recluse with billions, is offended and decides to go undercover to deal with the morons personally.

So many TV shows have played off the concept of an undercover boss, but this film is not a reality rip-off. It is a well-honed film from the classic period. Its politics and satiric approach are timeless.

On top of that, we were stunned in the opening credits with names like Edmund Gwenn, Spring Byington, William Demarest, Robert Cummings, and S.Z. Sakall. It is a who's who of brilliant character actors from the great studio era.

The opening and the closing scenes make the entire film worth the viewing.

The film even uses some of the *Citizen Kane* set, thanks to genius set designer William Cameron Menzies. And, Sam Wood directs comedy deftly. Heretofore, we associated him with social dramas that extracted stunning performances out of child actors.

In the final analysis the movie is not revolutionary or one of the great films, but it is something special despite its hoary sexism toward women. Yet, star Jean Arthur has spunk and is clearly engineering the road to independent women in business.

# Down Memory Lane

*William Holden*

When a friend bet me that the funniest TV show ever was on Amazon Prime, we could not resist to ask what it might be: she told us it was the old *Lucy* show with William Holden as guest.

Of course, we remembered it instantly, so indelible was its memory. It had to be fifty years since last we saw it on some endless loop of reruns that the show enjoyed for decades.

And, there it was listed as a 1954 episode on the third season of *I Love Lucy*. Free on Amazon Prime.

For those youngsters who have missed the wacky moment of one of the biggest stars of the 1950s showing up on a half-hour sit-com, it was something special back then. Holden was big.

William Holden had worked with Lucille Ball several times over the years earlier in their careers—and were good friends off-screen too.

So, his appearance was anticipated as much as John Wayne or Richard Widmark, who also did guest appearances that season—but Bill Holden's was distinctive and truly the epitome of the crazy red-head's "Hollywood adventures" when she went with her husband Ricky Ricardo for three months that year into celebrity heaven.

Her encounter with Holden at the Brown Derby restaurant turned into a spaghetti fiasco, with Holden winning a staring contest with the adoring fan. Upon embarrassment, Lucy beat a hasty retreat out of the restaurant, but knocked a waiter with a tray of cream pastry into William Holden.

Later, Lucy's husband (Desi Arnaz) brings home a surprise guest—none other than Holden. Lucy must don a disguise to avoid recognition. Her putty nose astounds as it twists one way and then another, ultimately aflame up when Holden tries to light her cigarette.

Yes, we counted about a dozen goodly guffaws, even years after knowing what was about to happen.

We can envy anyone who is about to see this little laugh-fest for the first time. Other episodes have been celebrated, but this Lucy episode was the one we truly loved.

## Tip Top Topper

We jumped into our Hot Tub Time Machine and transported ourselves back to 1937 to put on a mindset to watch the classic ghost movie, *Topper.*

Thorne Smith's novel has actually been compared to *The Great Gatsby* because the 1920s glamour couple (Cary Grant, Constance Bennett) seems to have stepped out of a Long Island party as the notorious George and Marian Kerby. They also seem ill-fated drivers. The original plan was to have W.C. Fields and Jean Harlow play the fun-loving Kerbys. What a movie that would have been!!!

Alas, the young couple is overplayed as self-indulgent, willful and spoiled rich folk by Grant and Bennett. They are neither witty, nor particularly likeable. If you expected this to be a set-up to how they act after they are turned into car crash dead people, you will not see Dead People.

Actor Roland Young is a surprisingly nimble and youthful old banker, adept at physical comedy, playing benighted Cosmo Topper. The Kerbys have their money at his bank and seem to bedevil him in life and want to be guardian angels in death.

Their amazing white Buick roadster (we presume it is white in a black and white world) actually crashes three times into the same spot during the movie, qualifying as a death car. Were the ghosts trying to transport old Toppie to the next plane?

Compared to the fancy special effects you'd encounter today in a residual haunt, the Kerbys are saving "ectoplasm," as Marian reveals. However, they appear alive and kicking in many scenes.

Billie Burke is perfect as Topper's wife with her confidante butler, Alan Mowbry.

The movie spawned a sequel, but neither Constance Bennett, nor Cary Grant, were around for that one. They said their goodbyes and went on to better scripts.

This film too often feels like dead weight to be a light-hearted comedy. Yet, by today's standards, it is worth 90 minutes of your time.

## Satiric Balletomaster

Korean dictator and koo-koo bird Kim Jung II have threatened war over a comedy movie by James Franco and Seth Rogan as two gayish CIA assassins out to get him.

It made us think back to another political satire that savaged a world leader. Charlie Chaplin took aim at Adenoid Hynkel (Adolf Hitler) in his 1940 film *The Great Dictator*.

Chaplin never shied away from big targets. It seemed to satisfy the size of *his* ego. If the Allies had lost the war, Hitler would have likely sought out Chaplin for a special place in the concentration camp.

*The Great Dictator* has some legendary bits among the funny scenes, but primarily one moment registers among the all-time great cinematic gems. Chaplin in the guise of Hitler dances a ballet with a large beach ball as the world. The choreography is flawless, funny, and horrifying, as Chaplin does his best Nijinsky imitation with global domination.

You know the world will blow up in Hitler's face.

As with all of Chaplin, his pathos outweighs his humor. If watching the faux Hitler and his double-cross insignia in lieu of the Swastika were not funny enough, he undercuts with his Jewish barber (his classic tramp role now with job). With coy Paulette Goddard, he fills in the dull parts with a dull love story.

Jack Oakie is around as the *faux* Mussolini to ramp up the competition among the dumbest dictators to give Chaplin a straight man when Billy Gilbert is not playing Herring.

In the era before the full horror of the Holocaust was known, the film simply put Hitler into the realm of deluded fools. It took history to open the full book on his evil. Yet, Chaplin's mildly acerbic portrait in an age when such satire was pre-American propaganda shows his sentience.

James Franco probably has no idea that he is playing on the same field with one of the greats of all-time cinema, though he'd likely warm to the notion.

## Captain Peacock and Mr. Humphreys, Redux

Derek Jacobi and Ian McKellen are among the royalty of acting, having cut their chops doing roles on *I, Claudius* and *Apt Pupil.*  McKellen is openly gay in real life, and Jacobi is relatively coy.

Now they have teamed up in their graybeard stage to play two mincing old queens living together for one of those amusing British comedy shows. Each episode is half-an-hour, and it is already on season two on British television.

We figured this series would not be Shakespeare (though McKellen's character is a former Shakespearean actor).

What we found ourselves watching in *Vicious* is a retread of the old hilarious comedy called *Are You Being Served?* We love that old show about a British department store and the delightful salespeople in men's and women's wear, which ran for eight or nine seasons and returned with the characters as elderly retirees for one last hurrah.

Plagiarism is alive and well. McKellen and Jacobi are elderly, openly gay, and living in bitchy humor land. They are also in the mold of the earlier series.

What we were unprepared to see is Derek Jacobi playing Mr. Humphreys, the fey sales clerk from the old show. He even has the tenor, the style, the speech patterns of the late actor John Inman. He must have studied the old reruns closely. And, the writers have stolen Mr. Humphreys always-unseen mother on the other end of the phone.

As for Ian McKellen, he seems to be playing Captain Peacock, the old show's floorwalker, now transformed into a pompous old stage walker. They trade snide insults and have stayed together for half a century.

It's the kind of show that could grow on one, but could also raise the hackles of gay political types looking for positive images of gay life with dignity.

There is little dignity in these proceedings, and precious few laughs too.

Must-See Leaf-Peeping!

Elaine May directed a handful of movies, and all of them went out of budgetary control. Her first, most successful film, taken out of her editing hands, was shortened by half its length. Some called it studio butchery.

Yet, forty years later, *A New Leaf* on a no-frills DVD is brilliant, frothy, irreverent, and a delightful adaptation of Jack Ritchie's macabre short story called "The Green Heart." Ritchie usually wrote for Alfred Hitchcock's magazine and had a few stories developed into series episodes.

So, Miss May intended a dark comedy indeed. It did not end up that way (thank heavens). Walter Matthau played a foppish elitist who loses his wealth and must resort to the unthinkable: marriage to a rich woman whom he would murder to gain her fortune and live his profligate lifestyle unimpeded.

May wrote, directed, and took the lead role as the helpless nebbish, Henrietta Lowell, rich and klutzy. An academic nerd with a good heart, she is gauche and louche. She played perfectly off Matthau, the only actor who could carry off Henry Graham with equal parts pathos and slime.

The first half of the movie simply carries the viewer along for a hilarious satire on a rich playboy facing penury. All this is assisted with a supporting cast of familiar faces and highly talented character actors, including George Rose, Doris Roberts, Jack Weston, Conrad Bain, and James Coco.

May's victim looks like a goner every step of the way, though the tables could be turned on those river rapids.

The film deserves rediscovery and deeper appreciation, even if it disappointed Elaine May. It will not disappoint the audience, and that will make this charmer a catharsis even Hitchcock must have enjoyed.

## Red-Faced Bad

Why did anyone want a sequel to the original comic adventure movie about retired CIA agents? We suppose it gave good salaries to its stars—Bruce Willis, Helen Mirren, John Malkovich, and now in the sequel, to Tim Piggot-Smith, Anthony Hopkins, and Catherine Zeta-Jones, all along for the long in the tooth ride.

Maybe they just wanted to have fun. Well, if your cup of tea is mayhem, and what dizzy funsters those old assassins really can be, this is your movie.

We hate any movie that is like a cartoon. This one revels in it. The opening credits, and the montages between scenes, are actual morphing into cartoon versions of the action and stars. This is DC Comics writ big, but with geriatric superheroes.

We knew that our tolerance level would be pushed to the limit with this little doozy. Usually we do not review films that we know will win our enmity. Perhaps for a few seconds, we thought this little dismal comedy thriller would transcend the materials. Call us wrong.

Perhaps we thought the aging stars would be hilarious in off-the-wall mode. Nope.

How misguided we were to entertain the notion something good would come this way. This movie is putrid for its violence and cavalier dispatching of human life. We don't find sociopathic killers among our favorite amusements. If that were the case, we'd be rooting for those laugh riot terrorists.

The film has excellent production values, easy to watch performances, and quick plotting. It's not enough. Trust us when we say that lugubrious movies with ponderous arty plots, like *You Ain't Seen Nothing Yet* and *Kill Your Darlings*, may be excruciating in their pseudo-arty approach, but we will take an effort to say something important over an effort to use chaos as comic relief.

Big budget failures are the worst—because the money would have been better spent in a serious (or humorous) little film. Sure, the producers may have to pay for a vocal coach for Daniel Radcliffe, or security for Robert Pattinson, but if the movie has merit, we applaud the expense.

*RED 2*should not inspire another *RED*. We'd rather have our stars go into genuine retirement than reprise these roles ever again.

## Instant Family, Minus Classic

Like castor oil, it's good for what ails you. So, we too take an annual dose of Jennifer Anniston to remind ourselves what the common folk like in movies.

Suffice it to say, we are dumbfounded as to why fans think a woman pushing 50, acting 30, should deserve their loyalty. To our surprise, Miss Anniston seems to be melding into a Maureen O'Hara-style career. She still seems much older than her leading man.

Her tough talking pole dancer turned Brady Bunch mother seems more akin to Barbara Stanwyck's comedy roles.

A group of drug dealers move up in the world to doing international drug smuggling under the guise of a family outing in an eye-popping RV. Of course, there are more f-bombs than your usual Marine drill sergeant might utter in a week.

These hard-nosed types will morph into your typical TV sitcom family of the 1950s (with an edge). It seems oddly funny except for the moral void at the core.

Jason Sudeikis plays the "father" and organizer of the drug smuggling operation. His character grows from a pothead to Fred MacMurray in a few choice moments, but the real star is born goes to Will Poulter as Kenny, the nerdy "son".

Put the typical nitwit humor out of your head because this film epitomizes nasty black-hearted satire, savage and unrelenting.

Blame all this on Rawson Marshall Thurber, the director, who had no choice but to go bad ass with a name like that.

## Unintentionally Funny

***Gilda Meets Kane in The Lady from Shanghai***

One of Orson Welles' final attempts at a Hollywood
mainstream production came with *The Lady from Shanghai*

,starring his then-wife Rita Hayworth. They were trying to be an early version of Burton & Taylor, but found they mustered closer to Sean Penn & Madonna.

The film has all the hallmarks of Welles, but worse yet, he plays a sailor with an Irish brogue that seems to have come from watching too many Barry Fitzgerald movies. We keep waiting for him to sing "Tura-Lura-Lura," that old Irish lullaby.

On top of that, Gilda herself is a bleached blonde. In those days, such a daring hair color change proved Miss Hayworth was more than a pretty face. She was an actress.

As for the big man himself, he takes turns either sucking in his gut or wearing a moo-moo shirt loose over the excess.

Many Welles team players dot the cast, including the delicious villain Everett Sloane as Bannister, Rita's well-to-do nutcase husband with steel braces on his legs--and the ever-familiar Erskine Sanford as the judge. Glenn Anders may sweat more diligently than any actor ever on film as Bannister's creepy law partner.

The movie is a treat of off-kilter camera angles and even more off-beat faces. All this was too much for studio-bound Hollywood production companies who wanted their movies with more matter and less art. Welles also created production furor at Columbia Pictures.

Whatever else the production became in fact and in legend, it is hypnotic like the proverbial train wreck. We become gawkers on the road to perdition, and it is entertaining to rubberneck.

The film ran nearly three-hours uncut, which is a tad long for a cheap noir satire, though you can still spot fleeting Errol Flynn near the yacht he rented to Welles for the movie. Flynn's pet dog, a Dachshund, steals every scene he's in, having learned well from Errol.

The movie's famous ending is the Hall of Mirrors extravaganza that is a hoot and a half. They don't make'em like this anymore. Actually, they never did make'em like this—excepting Orson Welles.

We still think this movie is high comedy, not melodrama.

Whatever Welles intended the story to be, it becomes a ridiculous crime *noir* to savor, reminiscent of *Touch of Evil,* which he would make a decade later.

# Making the Dead Pretty Lively

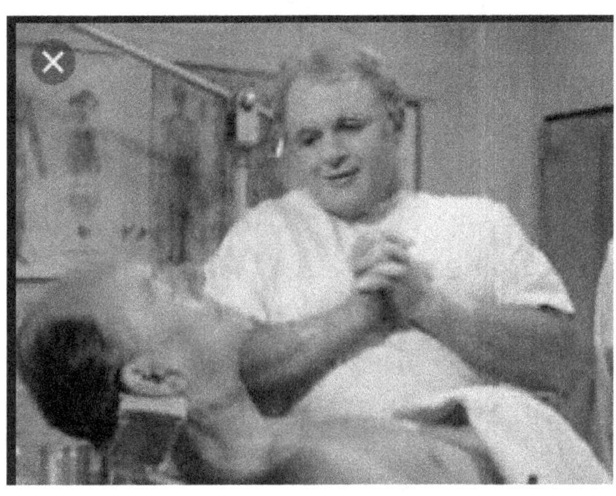

*John Gielgud played a dead man twice in 1965, here with his dedicated mortician, Mr. Joyboy (Rod Steiger) in a scene that has to be seen in The Loved One.*

Back in 1965, on the heels of *Dr. Strangelove*, dark comedy was all the rage.

So, Evelyn Waugh's *The Loved One* came to be produced. It was a scandalous tale about the funeral industry. And, it billed its tagline as the movie to offend everyone.

The first offense came with Robert Morse, a kind of all-American nerd who played a British national moving to Hollywood. He had so much trouble with his English accent that they had to record his lines and sync them in later.

The rest of the cast is brilliant—from Rod Steiger as Mr. Joyboy, an effeminate mortician, to Liberace as the coffin salesman. The roles seem reversed with those two.

John Gielgud played a dead body for the second time that year (first being in *Woman of Straw*). He proved to be a pliable and expressive dead man.

The end result resembles the end of Von Aschenbach in *Death in Venice.*

Other notables dot the entire production, making it fun to see the stars doing a cameo turn. Yet, the overall effect is neither offensive, nor witty. As written by Christopher Isherwood and Terry Southern, the tale seems full of sound and fury, written by the cottage industry scripters of the age.

Tony Richardson directed right off his highly entertaining and Oscar winning *Tom Jones.* He should have quit while he was ahead. But, to see Jonathan Winters in his young prime wanting to shoot the stiffs into outer space is worth every moment. He plays dual roles, becoming an American Peter Sellers here.

When an elderly British artist hangs himself as the studio fires him, his nephew has a Fellini *8&aHalf* trip to make the funeral arrangements. Actually the scenes in the Forest Lawn mockup look like *Last Year at Marienbad.*

The tour of Whispering Glades cemetery takes up a goodly amount of time to the strains of Wagner's *Tristan & Iseult* in a Disneyland for the Dead.

Black and white and black comedy all over, it won't make you laugh, but it will drop your jaw now and then. Whether you like it or not, or whether it is fine cinema or not, you should see it.

## Old Timer Comedy

*Grand Dame Eliz. Patterson!*

A long-forgotten movie from 1945 with Charles Coburn is called *Colonel Effingham's Raid.* It concerns a retired blowhard army officer who returns to his Georgia boyhood town to learn they are taking down the Confederate monument in the town square.

It seems ripped from today's headlines, but was a pop novel by Berry Fleming, another forgotten literary dim bulb of ages ago. It is supposed to be whimsical by standards of a century ago. Appalling would be a better word.

The notion that people would fight to keep up a symbol of racism in the Old South is played as a comedy! Indeed, black kids sit around and listen to the old white mayor praise the slave-owning South. Effingham hires black servants and treats them like basic training punching bags. Yikes.

One progressive woman (Joan Bennett) blames the corrupt mayor and his home-grown political party for hiring his "poor white" relations in town patronage jobs.

Effingham is a colonel in the general sense of Trump military leaders. Pompous and patriotic in an old-fashioned way, he will lead a pre-World War II Georgia town to rise in revolt to protect the Confederacy. How quaint, but it made America great back then.

The film is notable for its costars Cora Witherspoon and Elizabeth Patterson, two old biddy character actresses, as grand dames of the South. It also features the fake news media, up to its tricks for Trumpite Effingham.

If you want to see what made America 75 years ago, this hoary movie may be a rattling of your teacups. Ef-ing-ham is a satire, unlike his real-life counterpart in the White House, but both are ridiculous for sure.

## Blowhard Comedy: Classic Midnight Horn

For most of his career, actor and comedian Jack Benny blamed a movie called *The Horn Blows at Midnight* for ruining his movie stardom. In fact, he never made another movie for decades, succeeding on a newer medium called TV.

In some ways he was a re-actor, mostly playing off situations and people. Having a personality with notable quirks; vanity, greed, among his most notorious deadly sins, he was mostly asexual and devoid of anger issues.

Here he is faced with irony after irony: he drinks Paradise Coffee that 'helps you sleep'. He is too ineffective to start the doomsday scenario.

As a milquetoast, he was the antithesis of heroic post-World War II men--those tough guy approaches bordered on psychotic (all the major stars went from their usual roles to a more sinister version in the years after the war).

That bring us to *Midnight:* where and when Benny is a second-rate angel in heaven given the task of blowing Gabriel's horn (Heaven's real star's too busy) at midnight in New York City to end the corrupt world of a small planet called Earth.

It is whimsy gone mad. Nearly every joke is told twice. It almost becomes a Warner Brothers Bugs Bunny cartoon. Yet, the film was directed by action  helmsman Raoul Walsh. It used fantasy special effects and had a cast to die for. Yes, that is the original pantywaist Franklin Pangborn, and yes, that is Margaret Dumont from the Marx Brothers. Oh, yes, that is Robert Blake as a kid. Yes, that is every notable second-banana in second-banana roles. They are wonderful to behold.

It is not much more than a mild, simple whimsical tale with a few digs. Worse yet, the gimmick of the movie is blatantly false, which undercuts its sharpness. We won't tell you if Benny falls asleep too often.

It was not a bad film, but no one went to see it—and Jack took it personally. Of course, it does not help when Jack tells the audience that, if he saw this stuff in a movie, they would not believe it.  They didn't.

Benny retired from movies. His last starring vehicle is a diversion for the cynical, harsh times that followed World War II and the burgeoning Cold War. It also fits for us today in a mad, mad, mad world of Trump daily crises.

## *DATELINE: Chicken or Egg and Jack Benny*

Viewing *Westworld,*the new HBO series with its fascinating look at atomatons in an amusement park, we might be fooled into thinking how modern and futuristic the series is. But the possibilities were seen decades ago. Check this historical episode of the Benny series at the final 5 minute mark.

In the new Jonathan Nolan version of Michael Crichton's *Westworld* novel, there are now technicians running the theme park, wearing hazmat suits. In the old story they just wore lab coats. But working with robots nowadays probably is more hazardous, with their strange bodily fluids.

We were reminded that in the early 1960s, this same science-fiction premise was displayed innocuously enough on the Jack Benny Program.

Yep, the notorious tightwad comedian tackled the subject a decade before *Westworld* even happened.

In a 1963 episode young newcomer to TV, Johnny Carson visits Jack Benny in his dressing room after the show. He tells Benny how impressed he is with his style, energy, and youth. This, of course, just utterly charms smarmy Jack.

Coy as always, Benny is self-effacing. Then Johnny Carson asks him what the secret of his youth and vitality. It seems to bring Jack to a complete paralysis; he stares off into space. Johnny is alarmed as Benny never moves again.

Then a couple of technicians start to dismantle Jack, removing his head and arms and packing them away, putting his torso into the broom closet.

Johnny Carson is suitably shocked. He asks how long this has been going on.

The technicians shrug. They have no idea. "We started doing this 15 years ago."

# Two Lumps?

***Check Please.***

You have here a comedy of manners about the hellish life of a man whom everyone presumes is gay. This includes his mother and brother, and sundry supporting characters in the tale entitled *Coffee Date.*

You have here the classic misunderstanding and crossed identity.

Jonathan Bray certainly is an actor one might presume is gay. We know that his costar, Wilson Cruz, is a well-known gay actor who specializes in playing gay characters anywhere called upon. Here, he is a well-heeled owner of a beauty salon—and an excellent catch for anyone looking for a boyfriend.

Bray grows increasingly indignant and strident that no one will listen to his shrill protests too much and too often that he is straight (including to his ex-wife who insists she had nothing to do with his apparent conversion therapy).

Shirley Kirkland (coproducer and playing the smother) becomes increasingly unsympathetic. Bray's slob brother (Jonathan Silverman fallen onto hard times) sets him up with an Internet date with unknown sex identity named "Kelly."  Silverman's role grows more and more unbelievable.

NO pictures are exchanged on a truly blind online date, as if to heighten the preposterous nature of the film. When Bray meets Cruz, it is amusingly homophobic, but shrill as it continues.

There is some subtext about how a friendship can occur between a straight man and an adoring gay one. If the audience accepts the premise, you have low-brow Oscar Wilde and the importance of being earnest if not disingenuous.

A plethora of cheesy gay films has hit the streaming lists, leading one to wonder how and why they are made: usually about teenagers and first gay love & death. We are spared that tripe here.

We have steered clear of those irksome tales and sampled more mature characters in search of a purpose. This trifle boasts more staying power than most. It is more than tolerable. However, as per usual, we give our caution...

View at your own risk.

*Hunh?*

What have we got he-yah? When you go with a Channing Tatum movie, you never know what's inside the movie box of chocolates. *Logan Lucky* is pot luck and a spin of the wheel of fortune.

In this film, paunchy Channing looks like he put on 30 pounds from eating boxes of chocolates. It might be a fat suit, but on him it is a shock.

A rather extraordinary cast dumbs down their typecast Hollywood looks. We've seen these actors playing sharper and more sophisticated roles than the denizens of Hooterville in the Hills.

It's all in fun, though we aren't quite sure if hayseeds will be offended by the sincerity of the actors.

Channing Tatum and Adam Driver play a couple of down-on-their luck dumb and dumber brothers who are disabled veterans and abused and neglected good ol'boys.  One limps and one has a prosthetic hand.

Yes, it's a comedy.

This is the story of genuine brothers who don't need a bromance to seal the real deal.

You have to like them, even when Boss Hogg Daniel Craig shows up with a Southern drawl and platinum hair to tell them they are simpletons. They plan to break him out of the Big House to help them blow up a safe. For James Bond this is a grit of hominy.

It's part of Tatum and Driver's charm that they will use their abused lives to disabuse a race course speedway payroll. Hillary Swank is an investigating FBI agent.

Well, of course, we are in the deepest darkest land of speedway race-cars and going 'round the bend means a life of watching cars careen around a track several hundred laps.

These hillbillies make nice folks like the Clampitts seem like rocket scientists. When the brothers seek a computer expert, he boasts he knows "all the Twitters" with a twang.

The plot holes are in the heads of the characters. It's a caper movie with a twist of moonshine.

How could you resist this trifle truffle?

## Billy Wilder Classic

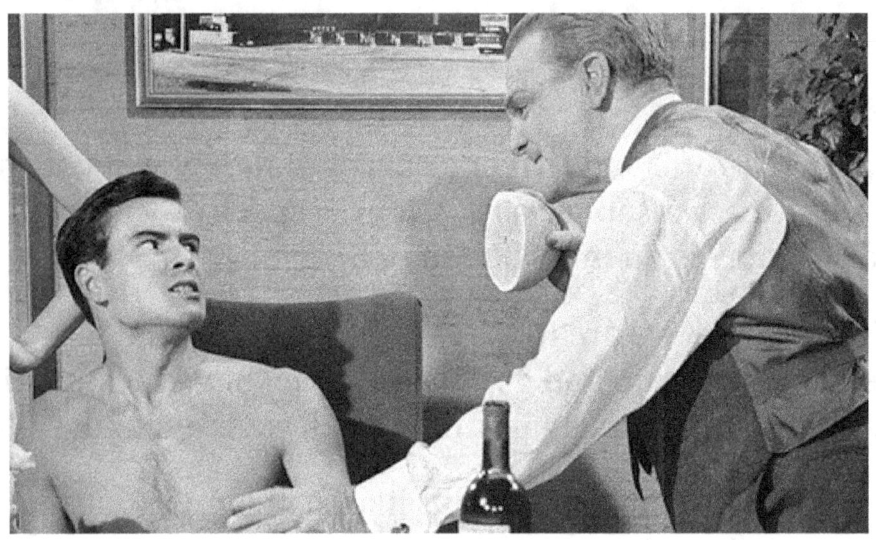

*Cagney reprises grapefruit scene.*

Topical political humor has a short shelf life, and you have only to see a few clips from *Saturday Night Live* in rerun to understand how quickly controversial becomes outdated.

When a major film tries it, as did Billy Wilder in 1962, only a few morsels remain fresh.

Yet, to take in *One, Two, Three*, the Cold War comedy, is less satisfying than say, *Dr. Strangelove,* which maintains its relevance.

When Wilder's outlandish satire was released, East Berlin put up a horrifying wall that changed history—and it was virtually ignored in the movie, except by a voice=over addition shortly before the film was released.

What survives in a favorite comedy is the manic performances.

James Cagney plays the head of Berlin's Coca-Cola division, unhealthy capitalism at its best, and he is marvelous to behold. He grows more intense with each passing scene, stealing anything he can make merry.

Others in the cast are less successful—but seem now perfectly placed in their roles:  game show actress Arlene Francis didn't forget her line was snide off-put wife. She is surprising effective, though the German jokes are thick.

Pamela Tiffin as the sex kitten from Atlanta is decorative, but she faded fast, unlike Ann-Margaret who might have run with the role. And, as her East German Commie boyfriend, Horst Buchholz sends out a post-James Dean vibe that shows how misused he was.

Leon Askin as the Russian commissar is delightful, and Lilo Pulver dances on tabletops in the Grand Hotel with lesbian couples while a hapless band plays and sings,  "Yes We Have No Bananas," in German.

The music of the intense and insane "Sabre Dance" is stirring to the break-neck pace of screwball comedy, already a dinosaur in Hollywood.

Cagney's version of *My Fair Laddie* turns a Commie lout into Austo-Hungarian royalty during the hilarious second-half of the film.  Cagney hated working with Horst and quit movies for years after. His best line to Buchholz who wants to lead a revolt of workers is: "Put your pants on, Spartacus."

You shouldn't miss it but brush up on your Cold War etiquette before tuning on the stream.

## Nothing Ventured?

*Big Moment on Film.*

All good things must come to an end, and there may be no more edgy way to end another collection than with our first viewing of Andy Warhol's 1963 salacious film called *Blow-Job.*

No one knows whether this was pure acting, or impure acting. Since more orgasmic porno is faked anyhow, we are sure that Warhol was keeping his secret. There is more edginess here than in a modern 21$^{st}$century real thing effort.

Don't get your knickers in. a twist. This film is the 27-minute version, and it is silent as well as black and white. If there had been sound, we may have accused the star of over-acting his role center-stage.

The star was a 24-year old actor who resembled James Dean, perhaps a fetish of Warhol. DeVeren Bookwaiter went out to do Shakespeare on stage and even appeared in the legit movie The Enforcer. We aren't sure how many jobs he won as a result of his Warhol notoriety. We never see the costar.

The film starts slowly before its inevitable climax. We suspect that foreplay may have enhanced the length—er, of the film. We see the main character only from his shoulders up, in a stylish leather jacket standing before one of those ubiquitous brick walls of New York.

Occasionally he looks nervous like he may hear the police siren closing in. For the most part, he moves around the film frame, and Warhol does not. So, the star often ducks into facial shadow, so we cannot see his bliss.

This could be a farce, or just a sex romp.

Now and then he throws his head back into the light of ecstasy. You cannot hear him, but several times he seems to say the word, "Yes," and near-on to 17 minutes he may shout out an epithet beginning with F.

The film goes in and out of a white blank, followed by the editor dots. It was either a second helping, or retakes by

Warhol. His camera seems to be having more fun the actor in question.

You know you are approaching the end when he throws up both hands and rubs his head. The real tell-tale sign that our break is near, he lights up a cigarette. On the whole, the film is fairly boring. Perhaps you had to be there.

We think he said, "thank you," near the end as smoke got in his eyes.

Well, that's art for you.

# One Singular Omission!

**Jimmy Kirkwood.**

The little documentary made about a revival of *A Chorus Line* is so warped by time and death that it is about as inaccurate as you can find when all the principals are long gone. *Every Little Step*  is really *Every Big Omission.*

Three of the creative forces behind the great musical play were Michael Bennett, Nick Dante, and James Kirkwood. They all died way too soon: and the survivors are allies of Michael Bennett (Marvin Hamlisch, Donna McKechnie, and Bob Avian). So, you have a slightly skewed presentation of the past.

I knew Jim Kirkwood—and he has been cut out of this film and you'd never know he had any role whatsoever for A Chorus Line (which happened to win him a Tony for writing and a Pulitzer Prize for good measure).

Cutting out Kirkwood from credit began while he was still alive. I can recall his complaint about how "hurtful" all this was—and he admitted to me he did have a physical altercation with Michael Bennett. I cannot imagine what that looked like—as Jim often advised me to "Kick'em in the nuts" to start and end any fight instantly.

Jim was proud of his contribution to A Chorus Line and even put the logo on his letterhead until someone complained to him about his "colossal ego." He removed the line of dancers and went with plain stationery. I told him to ignore such idiots, but he was overly sensitive.

This documentary would send him up to the roof and we might never get him down.

A great deal is made of the 12 hours of tapes of dancers' interviews that served as backbone of the libretto. Bennett recorded this one snowy December night in the 1970s, but Kirkwood insisted to me he never listened to a single tape. He read a transcript and had to give structure and order to it. He pointedly said to me, "There were no tapes. I never heard any tapes."

What intrigued him was his show biz background and literary themes of his life fit right into the storyline. If you read his works, you find every concept in *A Chorus Line* in books he wrote a decade earlier, from the Big Joker in the Sky concept of the "Director" to small details.

Even the biggest decision to change the ending to improve the book of the show is not given to Jim Kirkwood. It is entirely the idea of Michael Bennett. At the 1976 Tony Awards, Bennett gave a speech in which Kirkwood is mentioned as he gives "thanks to Jimmy."

The closing credits mention permission of the James Kirkwood Trust, but never is he mentioned within the documentary. Every Big Omission indeed. As a friend of Jim Kirkwood, I am furious about this distorted movie.

## George Sanders Loves Lucy!

Lucille Ball, George Sanders, Sir Cedric Hardwicke, Boris Karloff, and Charles Coburn. If you are an old movie fan, these names together in a movie will send you into the stratosphere. It's a murder mystery set in modern London with an American showgirl recruited by Scotland Yard to catch a serial killer.

*Lured* is a 1947 film overlooked by most because it is such a cross against typecast.

Lucy is sarcastically funny when she needs to be. George Sanders actually has a line in which he states, "I'm an unmitigated cad," and the killer has a penchant for the poetry of Charles Baudelaire.

This is not your usual mystery film. Douglas Sirk directs with his usual great aplomb and knows how to let his highly idiosyncratic actors play their stereotypes to the hilt. He made his name later in big budget soap opera movies, but here he plays *film noir* like a comic Hitchcock.

Not only that, the film is beautiful to look at—with its glossy black and white sets that do not scrimp on atmosphere.

Coburn is the lead Yard inspector—and his assistants are Alan Napier and Robert Coote!

The litany of rogue suspects is peachy Boris Karloff and Lucy are marvelous as he is the mad fashion designer and she is his model. Later she attends a Schubert concert after joining the staff of butler Alan Mowbray. She must hunt down each suspect with her brash comedy timing. You will soon recognize the Lucy you love.

You may not guess who the culprit is until the final reel—and Lucy does an excellent job working for Scotland Yard.

A lost gem, you owe it to see this charming comedy thriller.

# Who's Afraid of Insider Biography?

*Burtons with Nichols.*

Filmed shortly before his death several years ago, director and comedian Mike Nichols reviewed his life and career before an audience and in a more private interview. HBO put together this short film about Nichols called *Becoming Mike Nichols*.

The result is an illuminating exposition about a self-made director.

In the early 1960s in the heyday of the monologue comic standups like Mort Sahl and Bob Newhart, you had Nichols and May among the cleverest of all. Their run ended when, Nichols admits, he became too obstreperous director for May.

It opened up a chance to direct in theater, not merely his partner. He started with Neil Simon, Walter Matthau, Robert Redford, and *Odd Couple* on stage. Not exactly chopped liver.

He knew many Broadway stars from his years in New York, and met Richard Burton when they were in next door theaters. Burton later invited him to Rome to visit where he met Elizabeth Taylor while filming *Cleopatra*—and he was instrumental in having both appear in his first film, *Who's Afraid of Virginia Woolf.*

Three days before filming, he had friend Tony Perkins give him a crash course of pointers on use of camera in movies. In fact, he learned on the job. His work began a string of brilliant movies: *The Graduate, Carnal Knowledge, Catch-22*, and other literate films like *The Birdcage.*

The documentary focuses on his first two movies in depth, giving marvelous insights into Taylor, Burton, Dustin Hoffman, Buck Henry, and Simon and Garfunkel. The anecdotes leave the audience begging for more. A few pearls drop about Jack Warner, Billy Wilder, Anthony Perkins, but there is not time or attention to those.

There is nothing really about his Emmy winners or Tony winners. You may want to know about The Birdcage or Angels in America,  or his work on Gilda Radner or Whoopi Goldberg, but you will need to look elsewhere for that.

## Rarity, Rom-Com!

*Charming Cast!*

Oh, my, a mere trifle, a little movie satire of rom-coms.

It isn't brutal, but is gently sweet and it manages to convey its cynical attitude through the big girl Rebel Wilson as a wallflower overlooked by friends, coworkers, and society as a whole. She grows up learning she is not Julia Roberts.

We kept waiting for a new version of the classic tune *Isn't It Romantic,* that was the key song in its own movie in the 1930s and in *Sabrina* in the 1950s. Well, it never shows up, though there are several hilarious and giant musical numbers that give the entire cast a chance to show off skills not otherwise employed.

She is unlucky in love, and then is mugged: banging her head, to awaken in an alternate universe of romantic comedy, the film genre she despises so deeply. It's a movie stage version of her life, complete with musical interludes, a gay sidekick, and a wardrobe for the big size.

Throw in Liam Hemsworth as a billionaire playboy in counterpoint to the average nerd who adores her at work, and you have all the ingredients for a classic silly comedy. She fears she will end up in a slo-mo climax—and indeed, what she wishes not for.

Everything is right, not overbearing, and the sweetness is within the cursing cynicism of Rebel Wilson who decries this romantic version of the Big Apple and all the lovely people in it.

If you need a diversion nowadays—and who doesn't with coronavirus and masks everywhere—then this ditty will hit the spot more than ever before. We might have disparaged it a year ago, but today, we embraced its escapist charm.

Depending on how bad the news becomes, this movie will be nearby for a second viewing, the only antidote to the horrors of a pandemic.

## Old-Fashioned Murder Comedy

*Massachusetts mansion.*

The comedy murder mystery of the year, of perhaps the decade, is a Charlie Chan rip-off that is as trendy as it is traditional. *Knives Out* raises the question of why would anyone have a display of hundreds of knives in his parlor.

We think the set designer deserved an Oscar, or a strait-jacket.

An all-star cast of suspects seem to have as much fun making, perhaps more than those of us watching it. Director Rian Johnson moves his cast to the real star of the movie: a gothic house most suitable for his plot outside of Boston.

The lunacy of the house furnishings is like a Victorian nightmare, hardly something anyone would design, even an Agatha Christie murder mystery writer (Christopher Plummer) who hates movie versions of his books.

The family gathers for his 85th birthday—including his mother who must be 100 at least. And, the family members and staff are equally troublesome.

The cast even gathers for the reading of the will, which entails just about everyone—except the murder victim.

The best line delivered by Chris Evans is about cornpone Daniel Craig, playing super sleuth Benoit Blanc as "CSI- KFC,"  in shades of Sherlock with Hercule thrown in. But, we keep seeing James Bond slumming.

Director Johnson is utterly cruel with his camera. We have never seen these old stars looking so old. Every crevice, crease, and open pore, is ready for your perusal. Even Daniel Craig looks surprisingly aged in the wood.

The red herrings fly by at an alarming rate, so quickly it's hard to keep track of the lies and false statements. We suppose Plummer's nurse may be from Ecuador, Brazil, Peru, Uruguay, or Paraguay, as everyone cites a different locale.

The few scenes around Boston are amusing for those of us who are homebodies—and we snickered when Gary Tanguay, a Boston sports reporter, showed up as a news guy at another station.

It's a silly romp and more like what old movies used to be, and those Sherlock/Chan/Poirot stories were more succinct. We suppose there could be a new series for James Bond here if he so chooses.

## ABOUT THE AUTHOR

**Dr. William Russo has led more than three lives. He served as a college professor for several decades whilst moonlighting as a Hollywood historian, sneaking off to Burbank for late-night interviews with movie stars. Nowadays he works as a caretaker at a haunted house where its denizens amuse him with their cryptic antics.**